A
STRAIGHTFORWARD GUIDE
TO
EMPLOYMENT LAW

Karen Lee

Straightforward Guides
www.straightforwardco.co.uk

Straightforward Guides

© Straightforward Publishing 2013

British Library Cataloguing in Publication Data. A catalogue record for this book is available from the British Library.

ISBN 9781847163264

Printed by Berforts Group Herts

Cover design by Bookworks Islington

Whilst every effort has been made to ensure that the information contained within this book is correct at the time of going to print, the author and publisher accept no responsibility for inaccuracies contained within.

1

Overview of Employment L

The framework of employment law applies as soon as a j
Employers have legal obligations when drawing up a
specification and shortlist for a particular job. Essenti
employers must not discriminate against a candidate on
age, sex, race, religion or disability. There are laws to prev
any other factor such as trade union membership serve
you.

References

Prospective employers usually ask for references
appointment or prior to interview. References vary but u
employer should not provide a blatantly discriminatory
could jeopardise the chance of getting a job. However, tl
obligation not to conceal certain facts, such as reasons fo
courts have taken the view that the duty is to provide a re
substance true, accurate and fair. This was established in
Spring v Guardian Assurance (1994) IRLR 460 where
argued that a reference provided by a former employer wa
implied term in the contract of employment that any ref
compiled with all reasonable care. The House of Lords (
concluded that an employer has a duty to take rea
compiling a reference by ensuring the accuracy of the in
which it is based.

CONTENTS

Introduction

It is hoped that this brief, but wide ranging, introducti[on] law is accessible not only to the student but also to t[he] book attempts to embrace the framework of employmen[t] is brief introduction and concentrates more specifically [on] employee and employer.

Since the advent of the coalition government, there hav[e] changes in legislation, and also merging of legal departm[ents] also reflected in this book.

Throughout the book, there are cases that serve to highli[ght] law. There is reference to the 1996 Employment Rights [Act] into force on 22nd August 1996. This Act consolida[tes] existing Acts, including Employment Protection (C[onsolidation Act] 1978, Wages Act 1986 and Trade Union Reform and E[mployment Rights] Act 1993. In addition, following the 1999 Employment [Act the] 2004 Employment Relations Act now provides for enha[nced] Trade Unions.

The Equality Act 2010 replaced nine pieces of previous l[egislation, including] the Sex Discrimination Act and the Disability Discrimi[nation Act.] The Default Retirement Age been phased out which effe[ctively means that] employers cannot force employees to retire at the age [of 65, except in] certain circumstances.

Employment law has become increasingly complex and f[or those who] wishes a basic introduction and who wishes to know s[omething of their] rights this book should prove invaluable.

Application forms

When filling in an application form, it is clear that you should stick to the truth. In all cases, if it is found that you have lied when filling in an application form then that is a reason for dismissal. Few employers check educational qualifications and professional qualifications. This meant that in the past people were being employed to carry out jobs that they were not necessarily qualified to do. Companies now exist to check out CVs so honesty is the best policy.

Under the Immigration, Asylum and Nationality Act 2006 (which came into force on 29/2/2008), and which replaced the 1996 Immigration and Asylum Act, your employer must ask you for a National Insurance number or some evidence that you have the right to work in the UK. Employers have an obligation to carry out this check on all new employees. For employees who started work between 27/1/1996 and 28/2/2008 the 1996 Act applies. For full details of the kind of checks that need to be carried out and the sanctions against employers who do not comply visit the Home Office website on www.ukba.homeoffice.gov.uk.

Employers must also ask for criminal convictions. You do not have to reveal these if they are `spent'. This means that they happened long enough ago for the Rehabilitation of Offenders Act 1974 to allow you to keep them secret. If you are required to work with children or vulnerable adults, you will need to provide a certificate of disclosure. This is an official document which can be obtained from the Disclosure and Barring Service which has replaced the Criminal Records Bureau under the Protection of Freedoms Act 2012. It lists any relevant previous convictions More information about the Disclosures and Barring Service can be found on the Home Office website..

Also, your prospective employer must check with the police that you have no convictions regarding children.

As soon as you have accepted a job, you will enter into a contract with your employer, even if you have received nothing in writing. The basic terms of offer and acceptance apply. See Chapter two for more details of contracts of employment.

Other rights in the workplace

There are many rights (and obligations) at work, which begin from the day your employment commences. These are covered in depth throughout this book. To summarise a few of the fundamental ones:

Time off for public and workforce duties

All employees are entitled to reasonable time off to perform public duties, including serving as a magistrate or a local authority councillor. Your contract of employment may give you a right to paid time off for such duties. In addition, trade union representatives, union learning representatives, company pension trustees and designated health and safety representatives are also entitled to paid time off work to carry out duties.

Losing or leaving a job

Both employer and employee are entitled to a minimum period of notice of termination of employment. After one months employment you must give your employer at least one weeks notice. Your employer must give you at least one weeks notice after one month's employment up to 2 years and one week for every year after 2 years up to a maximum of 12 weeks, unless you are guilty of gross misconduct. Once you have had your job for at least a year, you can ask for a written statement of reasons for dismissal. You should be given one automatically if you get the sack while you are pregnant or on maternity leave.

The *Unfair Dismissal and Statement of Reasons for Dismissal (Variation of Qualifying Period) Order 2012* increased the qualifying period for the right to claim unfair dismissal to **two years** for employees whose employment commenced on or after 6 April 2012.1 Before this, section 108 of the *Employment Rights Act 1996* provided that employees had to have been continuously employed by their employer for at least **one year** to claim protection against unfair dismissal. In a variety of unfair dismissal cases specified by legislation, particular reasons for dismissal will be "automatically unfair". In these cases there is normally no requirement for a continuous period of employment.

Relocation of work

If your employer moves the location of their business, your situation depends firstly on the terms of your contract of employment. Some contracts include a mobility clause which says you have to move within certain limits. The notice period to move has to be reasonable as do all the other aspects of moving. You may decide not to move because of increased travel time and costs, moving house, family situation or children's education. If you don't have a mobility clause in your contract, and the relocation is more than a short distance, you can decide not to move. In this case, your employer may make you redundant. See Chapter 6, Being Made Redundant. When you are facing redundancy there is a right to a trial period in any alternative job that you have been offered. Redundancy is a dismissal so if you feel badly treated you may be able to claim for unfair dismissal.

If your employer decides to relocate:

- Check your contract of employment to see if there is a mobility clause
- Find out whether your employer is offering a relocation package and, if so, whether you think it is reasonable
- Discuss the matter of moving with your employer and state your intentions. If you decide to move talk to your employer about a trial period in the job
- If you decide not to relocate and your employer considers that you are being unreasonable and refuses you a redundancy payment,

you can take the matter to an Employment Tribunal (see Chapter 9) for them to decide whether you or your employer are being unreasonable.

Public and bank holidays

There is no statutory right to public and bank holidays as paid leave. This will generally be incorporated in your contract. Your employer may also count public and bank holidays as part of your annual leave. This is legal under the Working Time Regulations 1998 (see further in this book).

Transfer of a business

If your company is taken over, or if you work for the public sector and your job is transferred to the private sector, your terms and conditions of employment transfer automatically to the new employer. Continuity of employment is guaranteed. You have the right to raise objections about your contract being transferred to another company. However, this can he fraught with problems.

The transfer of contracts is known generally as the transfer of undertakings and is complex. Refer to the chapter on redundancy for more information. If you have a problem you will certainly need specialist advice from a union or other advice agency.

Sunday working

Certain groups of workers have protection in relation to working on a Sunday. They include shop workers and people who work in the betting industry. The aim was to allow those who do not wish to work on a Sunday to resist pressure to do so. However, if you have agreed a contract of employment that says you will work on Sunday then you do not have protection. Only employees who work in the above occupations have protection. For all other occupations, Sunday is just another day. There is also no legal right to extra pay for work on a Sunday although most contracts of employment will incorporate agreed overtime rates.

Insolvency of employer

If your employer goes bankrupt and cannot pay wages, the state will make up at least part of the pay. You can claim for statutory redundancy pay, wages up to a maximum of £430 (2012) for up to eight weeks. As well as basic ages you can claim any holiday pay up to 6 weeks, unpaid pension contributions and the basic award for unfair dismissal. You must apply to the employer's representative, usually the liquidator or receiver. You will be given a form which you should fill in and send off to the address on the form. HMRC will pay you any statutory sick pay, statutory maternity pay, statutory paternity pay and statutory adoption pay.

Suspension on medical grounds

In certain situations, usually for health and safety reasons, employers may feel obliged to suspend an employee from work on medical grounds. There are certain regulations under which medical suspension can apply - these usually involve working with chemicals or radioactive material or lead. There are also certain regulations in the Food Preparation industry which might lead to a suspension. This is because your Employer feels that you are a danger to your fellow employees!

Finally, if a pregnant woman is not able to carry out her normal duties, and no suitable alternative work can be provided, she can also be medically suspended from work.

If you are suspended from work on medical grounds in line with one of the qualifying regulations or conditions, then you are entitled to full pay for up to 26 weeks (as long as you have at least 1 months service). Any dismissal during this protected period is unfair. This does not apply if you are physically or mentally unfit for work. (If this is the case you will be entitled to some sick pay). It purely means that you are not capable of carrying out certain activities due to your condition. If you are offered suitable alternative work but refuse this, then no payment may be due to you. If your employer does not pay you, you can take a claim to an employment Tribunal, within three months.

10

Employment through agencies

Whereas once agency employment was tenuous, to say the least, all agency workers have some degree of protection under the 1973 Agencies Act. Recent legislation (Agency Workers Regulations 2010) has strengthened these rights. If you are working for an employment agency you may or may not be legally an employee. At the very least you will be a worker hired out to an employer to perform a service. Whether or not you are an employee, agency workers have basic rights:

All agency workers are covered by health and safety law, where the agency has a responsibility not to place you in a job for which you are not appropriately qualified and the company hiring you has a responsibility for providing a healthy and safe working environment.

-All agencies, and therefore agency workers, are covered by discrimination law, which also covers the hiring company.
-All agency workers are entitled to be paid the National Minimum Wage.
-All agency workers are entitled not to work more than an average of 48 hours a week unless you sign an agreement with the agency to the contrary.
-All agency workers should receive five weeks and three days paid annual leave once you have worked for more than 13 weeks.

Some agencies have been circumventing this by saying that your pay includes holiday pay and that they therefore do not have to pay extra if you take a break. It is unclear as to whether this is legal or not.

As an agency worker you may also be entitled to statutory maternity pay or paternity pay, depending on your earnings and how long you have worked for the agency. You are also allowed to join a union.

If you are an agency worker and you accept a permanent post then you are expected to work out a period of notice as an agency temp before becoming permanent. The company can also agree to pay the employer a lump sum to release you from your contract.

Other basic protections for agency workers are:

-You have the right to be paid by your agency, on the agreed day, even if the hiring company has not paid the agency.

-You must be consulted before any changes are made to the terms of employment or terms and conditions of employment.

Trade Union rights

A person has the right to decide whether they want to join a trade union or not. Employers are not entitled to know whether they are in a union. They should certainly not be asked questions at an interview about union membership, views or activity. Since 2004, Employers have not been allowed to offer incentives to an employee to leave a union, for example a higher pay rise to non-union employees.

If a person thinks they have been turned down for a job, or overlooked for promotion, because of their union membership or activity they should take further advice as this is a form of discrimination which is unlawful. The same applies if they think that they have been dismissed due to union membership or union activity. A special level of compensation is available for this.

A person can join any union of their choice, but obviously it is sensible to join a union which represents workers in specific jobs.

Employers only have to deal with a union if that union is formally "recognised" by the employer. This is a legal process which the union has to go through to get certain rights and protection. Views are more likely to be considered by an employer when the union is "recognised" by an employer.

Where the union is "recognised", the employer is legally obliged to discuss certain matters with the union, such as pay and terms of employment. Redundancy is another area that employers must consult the union on.

In certain circumstances a person is entitled to time off work for union meetings - but the employer does not have to pay when attending a union meeting. Some employers do give some paid time off to attend a union meeting, particularly when those meetings are important - pay offers or redundancy terms for example.

Representation

All workers now have the right to have a representative with them during formal disciplinary or grievance meetings. This can be a union rep but does not have to be. A person has the right to have a union rep with them even if the employer does not recognise any union. This is a right.

Trade Union Officials

As an elected representative of a trade union a person becomes entitled to certain rights and protection. A person can take paid time off to attend training courses and carry out union duties for example.

Strike action

Employees enjoy some protection if they go on official strike action called by a trade union. This protected period was increased to 12 weeks from October 2004, and it can be longer in certain situations - where an employer has made no attempt to negotiate, or employees have been "locked out" by an employer are examples.

A person is not protected against dismissal if they take unofficial strike action.

Whistleblowing

The general duty that confidential information must not be disclosed has always been subject to an important common law exception, that disclosure may be justified when it is in the public interest. The Public Interest Disclosure Act 1998 introduced new sections into the Employment Rights Act 1996 making it automatically unfair to dismiss workers or subject them to any detriment where they have made a protected disclosure. A disclosure of information is only protected where the worker honestly believes on reasonable grounds that it tends to show that a criminal offence is being committed, there has been failure to comply with a legal obligation, a miscarriage of justice has taken place, there is a danger to health and safety at work, damage to the environment or the deliberate concealment of any of these.

The Data Protection Act

Privacy at work is an issue which is gaining more prominence. Employers are in a position to collect increasing amounts of data about employees. The Data Protection Act 1998, amended by the Freedom of Information Act 2000, provides some important rights which people should be aware of. This Act gives Employees some control over information that their employer holds over them.

The Act gives all workers the right to be told about the type of information their employer holds over them, how that information is to be used and about anyone else with access to it. The employer must ensure that all information kept is confidential. Certain types of data, such as information about sexuality and religion cannot be kept. Employers can hold or use such sensitive data only in certain situations, such as when required to do so by law.

You have the right to see a copy of any information held about you, a right which has been broadened by the Freedom of Information and Data Protection Regulations 2004. The Regulations cover data kept on electronic or paper files. You can expect to see personnel files and other information held on file about you. The legislation also allows you to see reference information provided about you. An employer has an obligation to provide information promptly and can require a worker to pay a fee of up to £10 for producing the information.

An employee can refuse to disclose information if it means putting at risk a third party or requires disproportionate effort.

If any problems are experienced in this area there is the right to make a complaint to the information commissioner's office.

Monitoring at work

Most employers will carry out some form of monitoring in relation to their employees and this is accepted. However, where monitoring goes beyond the accepted boundaries of employee performance it needs to be done in a way that is lawful and fair. The Information Commissioner has set out guidance for employers in the Employment Practice Data Protection Code. Although the code is not a legal obligation itself, if your employer is not adhering to it he or she may be breaking the law on which it is based. For more information on the code of practice you can visit the website of the Information Commissioner at:

www.informationcommissioner.gov.uk

The Data Protection Act says that workplace monitoring must be justified by the benefits that the employer and others gain from it. Therefore, the code of practice suggests that in all but the most minor cases employers carry out an 'impact assessment' when deciding if and how to use monitoring. They must also consider whether monitoring is a proportionate response to the problem it seeks to address.

An impact assessment should:

- clearly identify the reason for the monitoring arrangement and the benefits it is likely to deliver;
- identify any likely negative effect of the monitoring on staff, including their private life within the workplace;
- consider alternatives to monitoring, or different ways in which it might be carried out with less disruption;
- take into account the results of any consultation with unions or staff representatives.

Knowledge and consent

Under the Data Protection Act, if monitoring involves the collection or processing of personal data a person should be made aware that it is being carried out and why. Employers who carry out a properly conducted impact assessment don't need the consent of individual workers.

The Default Retirement Age

The Default Retirement Age (DRA) was phased out between 6th April and 1st October 2011. The change gives people the freedom to continue working for longer. Employers, in the past, (and until 30th September 2011) could make staff retire at 65 even if they were fit and healthy enough to do the job. This could be achieved by giving six months notice to the employee. The last day employees could be retired using the DRA was 30th March 2011. Employers could still use the DRA between 30th March and 6th April, but had to use the 'short notice provisions'. Under these an employee could claim compensation (subject to a maximum of eight weeks wages)

Between 6th April and 30th September, only people who were notified before 6th April 2011, and whose retirement date is before 1st October, could be compulsorily retired. From 1st October, employers could not be able use the DRA to compulsorily retire employees.

There will still be exceptions to these new rules, however. Employers may continue to have a compulsory retirement age, but must be able to prove it is justified at an employment tribunal.

2

Employment Contracts-General Points

In the last chapter we looked at employment generally. In this chapter, we will look at employment contracts generally and in chapters 3 and 4 we will look specifically at terms of contracts and also implied duties within contract of employment.

When you commence work you may not be given an employment contract. The terms and conditions of your employment may be contained within a staff handbook. However, two months after employment commences you are entitled to a written statement of particulars of employment described below. This will set out the following:

- Your name and the name of your employer
- The date when your employment started
- Your rate of pay, when you will be paid and how the pay has been calculated. This must be at least the minimum wage. Sick pay entitlement should also be included.
- Your hours of work and holiday entitlement including public holidays. Both of these must provide the maximum/minimum under the Working Time Regulations.
- The title and description of your job and hours of work
- Your notice period
- The employers disciplinary and grievance procedure. (Whilst this was compulsory it is now optional)

You must also be informed in the statement whether the employment is permanent or fixed term. A fixed term contract will state when the employment comes to an end. However, the required notice is still due from the employer. Under new laws, if a person has a fixed term contract, the employer must not treat the fixed term employee less favourably than the permanent employee.

A contract of employment will use the terms 'employee' or 'servant' which distinguishes it from a contract of services under which an independent contractor performs services under contract for another person. Legally, the contractor is self-employed and the distinction between an employee and independent contractor is significant. Many Acts of Parliament and statutory regulations demand such a distinction. For example, part V1 of the Employment Protection (consolidation) Act 1978 (now 1996 Employment Rights Act) extends only to persons who are employees. Furthermore, the system of taxation is different as between self employed and employed persons.

In addition, the concept of vicarious liability normally extends only to the employer/employee relationship. Vicarious liability means that an employer is responsible for the legal consequences of acts done by his employees during the course of work. There are also certain implied terms, such as rights duties and obligations which are implied into every contract of employment, but they do not extend to self employed.

The question of whether the relationship of employer/employee exists is a matter for determination by the courts rather than relying solely on the description or label attached to the contract by the parties. In the case of Young and Woods v. West (1980): the Court of Appeal stated that whether a person is to be regarded as self employed or employed is a question of law not fact. The label which the parties attach to the relationship may be relevant to determining that relationship but it is not conclusive. The courts have developed several tests for distinguishing between employees and contractors.

The tests are as follows:

a. The control test. This test was formulated in the case of Yewens v Noakes (1880). Bramwell J stated " A servant is a person subject to the command of his master as to the manner in which he shall do his work" Does the person alleged to be the employer actually control the employee in respect of the work done and the performance of that work. If the answer was in the affirmative the relationship of employer/employee was established. In practice this test is largely redundant as working practices and societal norms have changed over the years.

b. The integration test. This test was first stated in precise terms by Denning LJ in Stevenson, Jordan and Harrison v. Macdonald and Evans (1952):

'One feature which seems to run through the instances is that, under a contract of service, a man is employed as part of the business, and his work is done as an integral part of the business: whereas, under a contract for services, his work, although done for the business, is not integrated into it, but is only accessory to it'

c. The economic reality test. In recent years the courts have used a more flexible approach which incorporates both of the previous tests. This is referred to as the economic reality test and means that factors such as control, integration and powers of selection etc are simply issues which contribute to the decision which must be based on all the circumstances. Held: there are three conditions which establish a contract of service:

a. The employee agrees to provide his own work and skill
b. There must be some element of control exercisable by the employer: and
c. The other terms of the contract must not be inconsistent with a contract of service.

In this case, a consideration of point (c) and particularly the question of the use of substitute drivers led to the finding that the driver was an independent contractor.

Recently, the tribunals and courts have tended to ask the single fundamental question: 'is the person who has engaged himself to perform these services performing them as a person in business on his own account'. Young and Woods V West (1980) is an important case in this respect. West worked for the appellants as a sheet metal worker, however choosing to pay his own tax and National Insurance. He had no entitlement to holiday or sick pay. Following the termination of his contract he claimed to be an employee and pursued a claim for unfair dismissal.

The Court of Appeal, applying the above test, said that it was impossible to regard West as being in business on his own account. Apart from handling his own deductions, and having no holiday or sick pay, West's conditions were the same as other workers.

One of the many problems arising out of the distinction between an employee and an independent contractor is that, particularly in the construction industry, workers are often taken on on the basis that they are self-employed, although, to all intents and purposes, they may appear employed. This is called the "lump" which means that the person contracting his services is paid a lump sum payment and takes care of his own tax, national insurance etc. The employer is absolved of responsibility for PAYE etc. Since 1971, legislative provisions have existed whose purpose is to minimise the income tax evasion through use of a system of exempting certificates available only to genuine sub- contractors. The most recent of these provisions are those contained in the Finance Act 1979.

Selection of employees

A number of statutory restrictions have been introduced which affect the employer's right to employ who he chooses. The main ones are the Disability Discrimination Act 1996, now replaced by the Equality Act 2010, The Rehabilitation of Offenders Act 1974, the Sex Discrimination

Act 1975 now replaced by the Equality Act 2010 and the Race Relations Act 1976 now replaced by the Equality Act 2010.

Rehabilitation of Offenders Act 1974

The 1974 Act allows a person to 'live down' certain convictions after a specified period of between six months and ten years, depending on the conviction and sentence, a conviction is deemed to be spent providing no serious offence has been committed during the rehabilitation period.

The Act provides that normally a spent conviction or failure to disclose it, is no ground for refusing to employ or dismiss a person or discriminate against him in employment. It should be noted that regulations under the Act means that it does not apply to a number of kinds of employment including teaching, medicine, accountancy etc.

Continuous employment

The concept of 'continuous employment is very important in that nearly all of the various statutory rights afforded employees are dependent upon the acquisition by the employee of two years continuous employment, as a minimum. The rules for computing the period of continuous employment are contained in schedule 13 of the Employment Rights (Consolidation) Act 1996.

Employment is presumed to be continuous unless the contrary is shown. Any week in which the employee is employed for sixteen hours or more counts towards computing the period of employment. These do not include 'hours on call'. Sickness injury etc does not discount weeks.

One vital question is: can separate concurrent contracts, with the same employer, be aggregated in order to give a person continuity of employment? In Lewis v. Surrey County Council (1987) L had worked for the council since 1969 in three art colleges. L had separate contracts for each college term and for each of the three courses. Each contract was confined to the particular department concerned. The contract merely specified the total number of hours to be worked. The House of Lords held that the contracts could not be aggregated as the legislation referred to only one single contractual obligation. The House of Lords did however indicate that L should have pleaded that the three contracts amounted to one single contract. Any week in which an employee is absent on account of a 'temporary cessation' of work counts in the calculation of a period of continuous employment. Any week during which an employee is absent counts towards continuous employment if, by arrangement or custom, the employment is regarded as continuous. Any week in which an employee is on strike, or absent from work because of a lock out, does not count in computing the period of employment but does not break continuity.

If an employee is employed for more than 16 hours per week and then becomes employed for less than 16 hours but more than 8 hours, he will, for a further period of twenty-six weeks, be treated as employed for more than 16 hours per week. If an employee has been employed for more than 8 hours per week, but less than 16, and has been so employed for five years, he is regarded as being continuously employed for that period.

Transfer of undertakings

There are various provisions dealing with the question of continuity of employment for the purposes of employment protection rights. The 1978 Act Schedule 13 and the Transfer of Undertakings (Protection of Employment) Regulations 1981 (TUPE) deal with these. The net effect of the provisions is that where there is a transfer to a new employer, continuity is not broken.

Specific employment contracts

Some groups of employees are in a special position with regard to contracts of employment.

Directors and partners

A company director is regarded as an employee for most of the statutory purposes if he has a written service contract with the company, but a non-

22

executive director is not usually regarded as an employee. Whether such a service contract exists is a matter of law, to be determined by reference to the facts of the particular case. Thus, even the director of a one-man business may be an employee.

One important case dealing with the employment rights of directors is that of Eaton v. Robert Eaton and Secretary of State for Employment (1988). Eaton was the managing director of RE Ltd. When the company ceased trading, he applied to the tribunal for a redundancy payment. No payment was granted as there was nothing in writing to indicate that E was an employee of the company and since 1981 E had not received any financial remuneration from the company because of its financial position. The EAT supported the decision of the tribunal as they could not find fault with the finding that E was a 'office holder' and therefore not an employee.

Partners

A partner in a firm is self-employed. If a person is employed by partners, the relationship of employer/employee exists.

Apprentices

A contract of apprenticeship is an agreement whereby the apprentice binds himself to the employer to learn the trade. Such a contract must be in writing (Apprentices Act 1814). The contract may only be terminated by the employer if the apprentice clearly demonstrates an intention not to learn or for gross misconduct. Conversely, the apprentice may only terminate the contract if the employer fails to provide instruction.

Although apprentices are entitled to claim statutory rights of unfair dismissal and/or redundancy, the expiry of an apprenticeship contract is not of itself unfair dismissal or redundancy.

Public sector employees

In the case of Crown servants, a relationship is enjoyed between Crown and employee which is analogous to a contract of employment, subject to an implied right of the Crown to dismiss without notice. Employees of nationalised industries and local authorities are not Crown employees. Unless an Act so provides, it does not bind the Crown. A number of modern employment law provisions, however, have been extended to cover the Crown.

Police

The police are excluded from many of the statutory rights to which other employees are entitled, e.g. the right to present a complaint of unfair dismissal. In addition, the rights of police officers to be members of trade unions and to engage in industrial action are severely limited. However, as 'office holders' police officers cannot be dismissed without a hearing and have a right to reinstatement in the event of the dismissal being found to be wrongful.

The armed forces

The armed forces are excluded from the various statutory rights enjoyed by employees. One of the questions which has been recently raised is whether or not a public sector employee is able to have the decision of his/her dismissal reviewed by the court through the judicial review procedure.

As the normal route of Industrial Tribunal cannot be followed by a 'office holder' e.g. a police officer, judicial review is appropriate to obtain a remedy as there is no alternative. The mere existence of a contract however will not stop a court from reviewing a decision where it thinks appropriate. One important case is McGoldrick v. London Borough of Brent (1987).

Minors

The ordinary rule of the law of contract is to the effect that a minor (person under eighteen) is bound by a contract of employment if the agreement as a whole is substantially to that persons benefit. In Doyle v. White City Stadium LTD and the British Boxing Board of Control (1935) an infant boxer held a BBBC license to box. After one contest he was disqualified and in accordance with BBBC rules his purse with- held. He claimed that the contract was not binding on him so the purse could not be withheld. The courts held that the contract was substantially to his benefit so the BBBC was within its rights to withhold the purse. In addition to common law there are some statutory restrictions covering minors. The Children and Young Persons Act 1933 and the Employment of Children Act 1973 regulate the employment of those minors below school leaving age (16). These Acts prevent the employment of any person under 13. Between the ages of 13-16 a minor may be employed in part time work subject to the restrictions as to the number of hours which may be worked and as to the time of such work.

There are also restrictions as to the employment in certain jobs, e.g. factories and mines. Between the ages of 16 and 18, minors are classed as young persons and in various legislative provisions restrictions are imposed upon the kind of work and the number of hours which such persons may do.

The Sex Discrimination Act 1986, now replaced by the Equality Act 2010, removed most of the existing statutory provisions restricting women's hours of work. Clauses 4-7 of the Employment Bill 1988 (now 1996 ERA) seeks to modify the differences between working conditions for women. Clause 8 seeks to repeal the majority of decisions relating to employment of 'young persons'. The aims of these repeals is to remove restrictions on hours and holidays.

Temporary employees

Once an employee has completed the appropriate period for continuous employment (notably one year for unfair dismissal) he is eligible to claim the various statutory rights. An employee who is engaged expressly as a temporary employee to replace someone suspended on medical grounds or absent on maternity leave is not normally regarded as unfairly dismissed when the absent employee returns.

Probationary employees

An employee may be engaged subject to a probationary period, the employer retaining the right to terminate or confirm the contract within or at the end of the specified time. Once the employee has completed the stated time he is eligible to present a complaint of unfair dismissal. As with any other dismissal, which is alleged to be unfair, the employer must show that he acted reasonably. Regular appraisals are seen as necessary evidence by tribunals in order to demonstrate that the employee under probation knew he may be dismissed.

Employees on fixed term contracts

Under such contracts employment rights depend on whether the contracts can be aggregated in order to give the employee continuous employment. There is no statutory definition of fixed term contract. However, following the decision in BBC v. Dixon (1979) it is clear that a fixed term contract is not fixed if it contains a clause for early termination.

A fixed term contract is one which expires on a particular date, rather than on the performance of a task or the happening of an event.

Fixed Term Working Regulations

The 2002 Employment Act implemented the long-awaited Fixed Term Employees (Prevention of less Favorable Treatment) Regulations which came into force on 1st October 2002. The Regulations were prompted by the need to ensure that British law complies with the EC Fixed Term Work Directives 1999/70/EC. In summary, the following are covered:

- Casual workers
- Seasonal workers
- Those on short term contracts
- Those employed for a specific task or project
- Those on temporary cover contracts
- Those on zero-hour contracts

A contract for a fixed period of time automatically terminates at the end of the period.

If the employment is for less than four weeks there is no entitlement, as of right, to a statement giving the main terms of employment or to any period of notice terminating the employment.

If the fixed term is for one year or more and is not renewed then the employee is treated as having been dismissed and a claim for unfair dismissal might arise, If the fixed term is for two years or more and not renewed then a claim for unfair dismissal might arise.

In essence fixed term workers cannot be treated less favorably than their colleagues who are permanent employees unless there is an objective reason for doing so.

Any intention to use fixed term contracts as a method of avoiding employment legislation will be carefully scrutinized by Employment Tribunals. Such a purpose is against the spirit of the legislation.

Government training schemes

The status of persons on these schemes depends on its nature. For example, Youth Training Schemes are aimed primarily at training as its objects are those of work experience and learning. Therefore a person on such a scheme is not an employee. Clearly, if a person is an employee under the scheme then service with an employer will count towards continuous employment. However, in schemes where the person is not an employee, previous training will not count towards continuity.

Persons over retiring age

The law in this area has recently been changed because of the European Court of Justice decision in Marshall v. Southampton and South West Hampshire Area Health Authority. (1986) This decision meant that the equal treatment directive was directly applicable to state employees, but legislation was required to provide a remedy for private sector employees.

The decision concerned men and women being required to retire at different ages which the ECJ held to be discriminatory. The response of the Government was to pass the Sex Discrimination Act 1986 which gave effect to the decision in Marshall but also made other amendments.

****

3

Employment Contracts-Terms of contract

Significance of the terms of contract

In any dispute between an employer and employee, the terms of the contract are of considerable significance in that one party may have a right to take legal action against the other in respect of any breach of contract. Of more importance is the significance of the terms of contract when an action for unfair dismissal is brought.

In such a case, although the question of whether one or more parties has broken the contract is of considerable importance, other considerations arise-notably whether the employer acted reasonably in dismissing the employee. Prior to the introduction of the remedy of unfair dismissal, an employer could always terminate the contract provided that he gave proper notice. The employee would have no recourse in law.

Sources of the terms of the contract

The terms of the contract of employment may be derived from a number of sources: minimum statutory standards; express statements of the parties; collective agreements; works rules books; custom; duties of employees; duties of employers.

It should be noted that, by virtue of the 1996 Employment Rights Act, an employer is under an obligation to supply his employees with a written statement containing information as to certain terms of the contract of employment.

Minimum Statutory Standards

In effect all those statutory rights and duties which apply to the employer/employee relationship may be said to form part of every contract of employment except those to which the statutory provisions do not apply. With very few exceptions it is not possible for parties to contract out of statutory provisions.

Minimum terms orders

Certain bodies, notably wage councils, are empowered to make orders which take effect as part of individual contracts of employment and are enforceable as such. It should be noted that the powers of wage councils were limited by the Wages Act 1986, itself consolidated by the 1996 Employment Rights Act.

Express statements of the parties

Nature of express statements. An express statement, in this context, is a statement, either oral or written, made by the employer to the employee (or vice versa) concerning the terms of the contract. Such statements may include letters of appointment, formal contracts drawn up by the employer, verbal statements as to the terms and conditions of employment upon which the person is to be employed (as to wages hours holidays etc) or other statements. If an express statement is made before the parties enter into the contract of employment, it forms part of the contract and may not be subsequently altered without the mutual consent of the parties. If one party deviates from the agreed pre-contractual terms, that party is in breach of contract unless the other consents to the deviation either expressly or by deviation.

Post-contractual statements. Post-contractual statements do not form part of the contract of employment unless the parties expressly or implicitly agree that such a statement does become part of the contract.

If an employee is employed upon certain terms which are not stated prior to the commencement of the contract and he is subsequently given a written statement which differs from the original terms the written statement does not supersede the written terms because the written statement is not to be regarded as contractual but merely as evidence of the contract.

Collective agreements

The term 'collective agreement' has a particular definition in s 178 (1) of the Trade Unions and Labour Relations (consolidation) Act 1992 but in general terms it may be described as an agreement between a trade union and an employer or employers association which deals, amongst other things, with the terms and conditions of employment of employees of the employer who is a party to the agreement. A collective agreement must be considered at two levels:

a) its effect as between the parties to it;
b) Its effect upon the individual contract of employment of the employees who are the object of the agreement.

It has been estimated that 75% of all employees have their terms and conditions of employment determined by collective agreements and it is therefore important to know the extent to which as a matter of law, such agreements form part of the individual contract of employment. This is sometimes referred to as the 'normative' effect of collective agreements. Several arguments have been advanced to suggest that a collective agreement must automatically be regarded as forming part of the contracts of employment of those employees to whom the agreement refers; but these arguments have generally been refuted by the courts.

The correctness of this view has been put under pressure by the Court of Appeal decision in Marley v Forward Trust Group Ltd (1986). M was employed as a field supervisor in F's Bristol office. His terms and conditions of employment incorporated the terms of a collective agreement with ASTMS, and included both a mobility and redundancy clause, the latter allowing a six-month trial period. However, the final clause of the agreement stated that the agreement is binding in honour only.

F closed their Bristol office and M worked in London, under the terms of the agreement, for a trial period. He found the job unsuitable and sought a redundancy payment. Both the IT and the EAT rejected his claim on the ground that the agreement was stated to be binding in honour only and was, accordingly, unenforceable. The Court of Appeal rejected this and held that the terms of an unenforceable collective agreement can be incorporated into contract so of employment and are then enforceable against the individual employee. The unenforceable nature of the agreement was limited to the parties to the agreement, in this case the employer and the union.

Express incorporation. It is fairly well established that it is possible to incorporate a collective agreement into an individual contract of employment if the contract expressly provides that this is to be the case. In National Coal Board v Galley (1958) it was held that a clause of a collective agreement which stated that colliery deputies would work 'such days or part days in each week as may reasonably be required by the employer' could be regarded as being part of the original contracts of employment because the contracts of the deputies referred to that collective agreement as being the source of the terms of the contracts.

It should be noted that the written statement supplied pursuant to the 1992 Act permits the employer to refer an employee to a document, such as a collective agreement, as being the source of certain terms of the contract of employment. A Collective agreement may also expressly become part of a contract of employment by virtue of statutory provisions. There are a number of situations where this is possible:

a) under the 1992 Act. Provision is made for application to be made to the Secretary of State for the approval of dismissals procedures agreements.

Such agreements, which replace the right to claim unfair dismissal for those employees covered, form part of the terms of employment of those employees within their ambit;

b) under the 1992 Act, a collective agreement may be made which substitutes for the right to claim a redundancy payment under the provisions of the 1996 Act, a right to claim under the collective agreement If such an agreement approved by the Secretary of State, it forms part of the terms of employment of those employees to whom it applies;

c) under the 1992 Act a collective agreement may be made which substitutes for the right to a guarantee payment under the provisions of the 1996 Act, a right to claim under the collective agreement. It should be noted that where the terms of a collective agreement are expressly incorporated and varied by consent between the unions and employers the new terms become incorporated into the individual contracts of employment; however, unilateral variation or abrogation of the agreement by one party does not have a corresponding effect on individual employment contracts (Robertson A and Jackson v British Gas (1983).

Works rule-books

A works rulebook can take a number of forms in so far as it may consist of an actual book given to each employee when he enters employment or at some subsequent date. These rules relate to disciplinary action, suspension, dismissal for conduct etc. Safety procedures are normally incorporated. S.3 of the Employment Rights Act 1996 states that an employer must give details of disciplinary and grievance procedures to an employee when taking up employment.

As far as the effect on contract goes, if the employer gives the employee the rulebook, or expressly refers to it before a contract is signed then it is considered to be part of the contract. In Petrie v Macfisheries (1940) a notice was posted on the wall of the work place stating the circumstances in which sick pay would be paid. The plaintiff claimed that it was not part of his contract. The defendant's case was upheld as the rule concerning sick pay was deemed to be incorporated into his contract as a result of his continued working at the place.

Not all works rules will be part of the contract, particularly where there are numerous rules contained in the relevant documentation, some for example may be out of date and inappropriate. This is well illustrated by the decision in Secretary of State for Employment v ASLEF (1972) a case concerning the rule book of British Rail, where Lord Denning said ' Each man signs a form saying that he will abide by the rules but these rules are in no way terms of the contract of employment. They are only instructions to a man as to how to do his work'.

Custom

Custom plays a significant part in employment law. It seems that there are four different categories of custom, which may form part of a contract of employment.

a) Custom of a particular place of work.

b) Custom of an industry or trade.

c) Custom of a specific geographical locality.

d) Customary conduct of the parties to the contract of employment.

a) See Marshall v English Electric !1945)

b) See Sagar v Ridehalgh (1931) and Davson v France (1959)

c) Sagar v Ridehalgh

d) Mears v Safecar Security (1982)

4

Employment Contracts-Implied Duties of the Employer/Employee

Into every contract of employment are implied a number of obligations in so far as these are not inconsistent with the express terms of the individual contract of employment. These duties are based on principles developed by the courts in the decided cases.

Implied duties may be classified as follows:
a) to be ready and willing to work;

b) to use reasonable care and skill;

c) to obey lawful orders;

d) to take care of the employers property;

e) to act in good faith.

To be ready and willing to work
The fundamental duty owed to an employer by an employee is to be turn up to work and to work at the direction of the employer in return for wages. Two interesting cases have arisen in relation to this. In Miles v Wakefield Metropolitan District Council (1987) M was a superintendent registrar of births deaths and marriages, working 37 hours per week, three

of which were on Saturday morning. As part of industrial action, M refused to carry out marriages on Saturday mornings, although he was willing to do his other work. Wages were deducted, M sued for lost wages and the employer won, with the House of Lords (Supreme Court) saying that where an employee refuses to perform the full range of duties and had been told that he would not be paid if he did not, then the employers were entitled to withhold the whole of his remuneration, (3hrs) although he attended for work and carried out a substantial part of his duties.

To use reasonable care and skill
This has two aspects:
a) The duty not to be unduly negligent.
b) The duty to be reasonably competent.

If an employee is negligent during the course of his work, he may be regarded as being in breach of contract. In Lister v Romford Ice and Cold Storage Ltd (1957) a lorry driver, employed by the company, carelessly reversed his lorry and injured a fellow employee, who was his father. The employers paid damages to the father but claimed indemnity from the son, because of negligence. This was held to be the case.

Duty to be reasonably competent
If an employee is incompetent this may be a breach of contract. In Hamer v Cornelius (1858) this was held to be the case.

To obey lawful orders
An employee is under a duty to obey all the lawful orders of his employer, i.e. those which are within the scope of the contract. In Price v Mouat (1862) a lace salesman was ordered to card (pack) lace but he refused and was dismissed without notice. He claimed wrongful dismissal and this was held because the order was not one which was within the scope of his contract.

36

An employee, therefore, is not obliged to do any act, which is deemed to fall outside the ambit of his individual contract of employment. The question of the introduction of new technology has caused problems here and must be linked to the scope of managerial prerogative in introducing new work techniques. In Cresswell v Board of Inland Revenue (1984) the Revenue wished to introduce a computer system to assist with the PAYE system. The majority of the work associated with the system had been done manually. Did the employers have the ability to change the nature of the working system? Did the employers have the ability to change the nature of the working system? Held: employees were expected to adopt the new methods and techniques in performing their contracts if the employer provided the necessary training in new skills.

To take care of employers property

An employer is under an obligation to take reasonable care of his employer's property. In Superflux v Plaisted (1958) the defendant had been in charge of a team of vacuum cleaner salesmen and had negligently allowed fourteen cleaners to be stolen from his van. Held: he was in breach of his contract of employment.

To act in good faith

His implied duty has several different aspects, which together form the basis of a relationship of trust. There is the duty not to make a secret profit, i.e. not to accept bribes.

This principal was clear from the case of Reading v AG (1951) which concerned a member of the armed forces, in which Lord Normand said:

---though the relation of a member of his majesty's forces is not accurately described as that of a servant under a contract of service--he owes to the Crown a duty as full fiduciary as the duty of a servant to his master--and in consequence--all profits and advantages gained by the use of his military status are to be for the benefit of the Crown'.

Duty to disclose certain information.

There appears to be no general duty on an employee to inform his employer of his misconduct and deficiencies: Bell v Lever Brothers (1932). However, there is one important exception, namely where the employment of that particular person is made more hazardous by virtue of an undisclosed defect on part of the employee.

Covenants in restraint of trade

A covenant in restraint of trade is a clause in a contract, which purports to limit an employees rights to seek employment when and where he chooses upon leaving his employment. This is usually done as a protective measure by an employer when he might suffer as a result of disclosure of confidential information or for other such reasons.

There are difficulties however, in enforcing such covenants and the employer has to demonstrate that the covenant is justified. A court will look at such factors as the time that the covenant runs, geographical area that it covers and public interest when considering the reasonableness of such covenants.

If a covenant is found to be unreasonable, the contract as a whole is not necessarily regarded as void, unless it is impossible to distinguish the covenant from the rest of the contract. If the covenant can be severed from the rest of the contract, without altering the nature of the agreement, the unreasonable clause may be struck out: see Commercial Plastics LTD v Vincent (1965).

If an employer breaks the contract of employment by wrongfully dismissing an employee, the employee may disregard any covenant in the contract which purports to limit his right to seek employment elsewhere: see General Billposting v Atkinson (1909).

Patents

At common law, unless the contract dealt with the matter, an employee would not normally be entitled to the benefit of any invention made by him if to allow him to do so would be a contravention of the implied duty of the employee to act in good faith.

The Patents Act 1977, ss-39-47, gives ownership of an invention to the employee inventor unless the invention was made in the course of the duties for which he was employed. Any disputes are dealt with by the patents court.

Duties of the employer

By virtue of common law, and a number of statutory provisions, employers have a considerable number of obligations towards employees. The main examples are:

To pay contractually agreed remuneration

An employer is under no obligation to provide work as long as remuneration is paid. This however, has been questioned in recent times, particularly in relation to skilled employees. Lord Denning said, in Langston v AUEW (1973): 'In these days an employer, when employing a skilled man, is bound to provide him with work. By which I mean that the man should be given the opportunity of doing his work when it is available and when he is ready and willing to do it'. Therefore, a failure to provide work of a nature that the employee is used to could be regarded as constructive dismissal.

There are three exceptions to the rule, one is piecework, the second is where the nature of the employment is such that the actual performance of the work forms part of the consideration supplied by the employer, the employee may be entitled to compensation over and above the contractual wages. These situations are sometimes referred to as 'names in lights' clauses. the other exception is when an employee is taking part in limited industrial action.

National Minimum Wage

From April 1999 the amount of pay an employee is entitled to receive is governed by the National Minimum Wage Act (NMW) 1998.

The Act by s.1 covers worker's which is wider than the traditional definition of employee in employment law. Essentially, the NMW will apply to a workers gross pay, which will include incentive payments. Certain other benefits will be excluded from the calculation, such as tips.

From October 2012 the main adult rate for workers aged 21 and over is be £6.19 per hour. The rate for worker 18-20 is £4.98 per hour. For workers aged 16-17 the rate is £3.68 Apprentices £2.65 per hour..

The above figures are correct at the time of writing. For up to date figures and other information concerning the NMW contact ACAS through their website or the Pay and Work Rights Helpline on 0800 917 2368.

The following groups are not entitled to the National Minimum Wage:

- self-employed people
- company directors
- volunteers or voluntary workers
- workers on a government employment programme, eg the Work Programme
- family members of the employer living in the employer's home
- non-family members living in the employer's home who share in the work and leisure activities, are treated as one of the family and aren't charged for meals or accommodation (eg au pairs)
- workers younger than school leaving age (usually 16)
- higher and further education students on a work placement up to 1 year
- workers on government pre-apprenticeships schemes
- people on certain European Union programmes
- people working in a Jobcentre Plus Work trial for 6 weeks
- members of the armed forces
- share fishermen
- prisoners
- people living and working in a religious community

Work experience and internships

You won't get minimum wage if you're:

- a student doing work experience as part of a higher education course
- of compulsory school age (usually 16)
- a volunteer or doing voluntary work
- on a government or European programme
- work shadowing

Voluntary work

You're classed as doing voluntary work if you can only get certain limited benefits (eg reasonable travel or lunch expenses) and you're working for a:

- charity
- voluntary organisation or associated fund-raising body
- statutory body

Pay reference period

The NMW is set at an hourly rate but that does not mean you must be paid at least the NMW for each hour you work. Rather, your average hourly pay must be at least the NMW as worked out over the 'pay reference period'. The pay reference period is the interval between which you are normally paid. If you are normally paid on a daily basis your pay reference period is one day, if you are paid weekly it will be one week and if monthly, one month.

Your pay reference period cannot be longer than one month. If you are normally paid quarterly, you have a right to be paid at least the NMW on average during each month within that quarter. Most people can easily work out whether they are getting the NMW by dividing their pay (before tax and other permitted deductions by the number of hours worked.

Permitted deductions

Your employer is legally required to make the following deductions from your pay:

- Income tax
- National Insurance
- Student loan payments
- Pension contributions
- Trade union subscriptions

There are certain payments and deductions that do not count towards your NMW pay. These include deductions and payments made by your employer for:

-Tools, uniforms etc. which you employer provides for you to do your job
-Expenses paid to you for costs incurred in your job
-Goods and services connected to your employment which your employer retains for their own use and benefit, such as the use of transport to and from work.

It is unlawful for employers to make such deductions or require you to make such payments if it means that you do not receive the NMW.

From 2009 onwards it is unlawful for employers to count tips or gratuities you receive from customers towards your NMW pay. In addition, any premiums of pay which you receive on top of basic rate for working at special times are not counted along with any other special allowances.

Benefits in kind also cannot count towards the NMW. The only exception is a set amount for accommodation. Examples of benefits in kind can be meals, staff car, medical insurance, gym membership, lunch vouchers, childcare vouchers, eye test vouchers and employers contributions towards a pension.

To treat employees with trust and confidence

In Courtaulds Northern Textiles Ltd v Andrew (1978) the EAT held'--- there is an implied term in a contract of employment that employers will not, without reasonable and proper cause, conduct themselves in a manner calculated or likely to destroy or seriously damage the relationship of trust or confidence between the parties' A series of cases have firmly established this principle.

To observe provisions relating to holidays

The written statement provided to employees under the 1996 Act ought to state the holidays to which the employee is entitled and whether the employee is entitled to holiday pay and if so how much. There are relatively few statutory provisions. Section 94 of the Factories Act 1961 provides that women and young persons who work in factories must have a holiday on bank holidays and the Wages Councils and Agricultural Wages Board have the power to fix holiday pay for workers in the industries over which they have jurisdiction.

To observe provisions relating to hours of work

The hours which an employee is required to work are determined by reference to his individual contract of employment and the written statement supplied to the employee ought to state these. There are certain statutory provisions, section 7 of the Sex Discrimination Act 1986 (now replaced by the Equality Act 2010) removed the majority of limitations imposed concerning the hours to be worked by women. Part V1 of the Factories Act 1961 limits the working day to no more than nine hours for young people.

In addition, see below, the Working Time Regulations 1998. These have introduced specific regulations controlling the working week and covers a broad variety of workers not only employees.

43

To permit employees time off work for public duties

The 1996 Act provides that an employer must permit an employee to have time off work for the purpose of carrying out work as:

a) Justice of the peace (work relating to this)
b) a member of a local authority
c) a member of a statutory tribunal
d) a member of a regional health authority or an Area or District educational establishment.
e) a member of a governing body of a local authority maintained educational establishment.

A number of categories of employees are excluded from this right, under the 1996 Act. Under the 1996 Act a pregnant employee has the right not to be unreasonably refused time off work with pay in order that she may keep appointments for receiving anti-natal care. Evidence of pregnancy and appointment must be produced if requested by employer.

To indemnify employees

An employer is under an obligation to indemnify his employees in respect of any expenses incurred in performing their duties under the contract of employment, for example traveling expenses. In certain circumstances however, the employee may be under an obligation to indemnify the employer for any loss sustained: see Lister v Romford Ice and Cold Storage LTD (1957)

To provide references

There is no obligation on an employer to supply character references for employees although, in practice, employers normally supply them since failure to provide one speaks for itself. The legal effect of references means that if an employer does provide one, it ought to be correct for several reasons: If a reference is defamatory, the defamed employee may bring an action against the employer, although the defence of qualified privilege is available to the employer, i.e. the employer may show that the statements were made without malice.

Negligent misstatement. A person who acts in reliance on a reference, which has been issued negligently, may apparently bring an action to recover any loss sustained as a consequence.

Working Time Rights
Under Europe's Working Time Directive, most people now have seven basic rights to proper time off, rest breaks and paid holiday.

Who has working time rights?
These working time rights apply to all employees and workers from the first day of employment. The rights apply to most agency workers, homeworkers and freelancers. Only those who are self-employed and are genuinely running their own business do not have the right to paid annual leave.

Working time rights do not apply to:
- individuals who are self-employed and who are genuinely running their own business
- individuals who can choose freely their hours and duration of work (such as a managing executive)
- the armed forces, emergency services and police are excluded in some circumstances
- domestic servants in private houses

Working time rules also apply differently to some groups of workers (e.g. those who have to travel a long distance from home to get to work) and in some sectors or workplaces (e.g. security, hospitals, or air, road or sea transport) or when there is an emergency or accident.

Rest breaks

You have the right to a rest break of at least 20 minutes where you work for a continuous period of six hours or more during a working day / shift. If you are under 18 however, you are entitled to a 30-minute break after working four and a half hours.

Additional or longer breaks may be provided for in your contract. A lunch break or coffee break can count as a rest break.

The requirements are:
- the break must be in one block
- it cannot be taken off one end of the working day - it must be somewhere in the middle
- you are allowed to spend it away from the workplace

Your employer can say when rest breaks can be taken provided they meet these requirements.

You do not have an automatic right to be paid for rest breaks. Whether you receive pay for rest breaks will depend on your contract.

Daily rest periods

You have the right to a rest period of 11 uninterrupted hours every working day.

If you are under 18, you are entitled to a 12 hour uninterrupted rest period per working day.

This rest period must be continuous and uninterrupted.

Weekly rest breaks

You have the right to a rest period of either:
- 24 hours in every 7 day period or

46

- 48 hours in every fortnight

This rest period must be continuous and uninterrupted.

Employers have a duty to make sure that you take your breaks.

48 hour working time limit

You have the right not to work more than 48 hours a week on average. This limit is averaged over a 17-week period. This means that it is legal to work more than 48 hours in some weeks, so long as you work less in others.

You can opt out of this right unless you work at night, but should not be pressured to opt out. The opt-out must be voluntary and must be in writing.

You have a right to opt back in again to working time protection at anytime, but you must give your employer at least 7 days notice. You may be required to give more notice - up to 3 months, if you previously agreed to this with your employer in writing.

Young workers and working time limits

The weekly working time limits for young workers are 8 hours a day and 40 hours per week.

For the majority of young workers these are absolute limits. A young worker's working time is not averaged over a reference period, so in one week they must not work more than 40 hours. The opt-out provisions do not apply to young workers. Please see the section below.

Young workers will only be able to work more than 8 hours per day, or 40 hours per week if they are needed to:

- keep the continuity of service or production
- respond to a surge in demand for a service or product

And provided that:

- there is no adult available to do the work
- their training needs are not negatively affected

For further detailed information about your working time rights and how these can be enforced please see the TUC guide, 'Enforcing your Basic Workplace Rights'.

What counts as working time?

As well as time spent doing your job, your working time will include time spent on:

- job related training
- job related travelling time, although not time spent travelling
- overtime, whether paid or unpaid
- time spent 'on-call' at the workplace
- working lunches
- time spent working abroad if you work for a UK- based company

What does not count as working time?

Your working time does not include:
- breaks when no work is done, e.g. lunch breaks
- time when you are on-call away from the workplace (although time spent working when away from the workplace, e.g. answering calls at home, will count as working time)
- paid or unpaid holidays

Working in more than one job

If you work for more than one employer, the combined time that you work should not exceed more than 48 hours, unless you have signed the opt out with your employers.

Night work

Regular night workers should not work more than eight hours in each 24-hour period. The Working Time Regulations allow for night work to be averaged over a 17-week period in the same way as weekly hours of work. Please note that there is no opt out from the night work limits.

If your night work involves special hazards or heavy physical or mental strain, you cannot be made to work more than eight hours in any 24 hour period.

Young workers under 18 are not permitted to work between 10pm-6am.

Before night work can commence an employer must have offered you an opportunity to undertake a free health assessment unless you have previously had a health assessment which is still valid.

Your employer must then offer you free health assessments at regular intervals, to ensure it is still safe for you to undertake night work.

Where an employer is advised by a doctor/registered medical practitioner that you cannot undertake night work, the employer should where possible, transfer you to work which they are suited and is work within normal working time (day time).

It is good practice for your employer to provide you with enhanced pay rates for doing night work or unsocial hours. But you will not have a right to receive enhanced pay for doing night work, unless your contract provides for it.

What can I do if I am not allowed to take rest breaks or am asked to work excessive hours?

If your employer does not permit you to take rest breaks or daily or weekly breaks, you can make a complaint to an Employment Tribunal.

If your employer pressurises you to work more than 48 hours when you have not signed an opt-out or does not comply with night work rules, you can make a complaint through the Pay and Work Rights helpline.

It is always a good idea to seek advice from your union rep or from the ACAS Helpline before taking steps to enforce your rights.

For more information please go to the section on enforcing your rights.

Holiday pay

If you work regular hours and get the same pay each week, then holiday pay is simply the same as your normal pay. If your normal pay includes regular bonuses, shift premiums or contractual overtime payments, then these should also be included in your holiday pay.

If your weekly pay varies because your hours vary from week to week, then your weekly holiday pay should be the average weekly pay you earned over the last 12 weeks.

Holiday pay paid throughout the year

When paid holidays were first introduced in 1998, some people found a change to their pay slip. Their take home pay was still the same, but now made up of two elements. First was their basic pay, which had been reduced from what it had been in previous pay packets. The difference was made up with a new element called holiday pay. The employer then said that there was no need for paid holidays as you were getting your holiday pay throughout the year and should save up for it.

Paying holiday pay in this way is now illegal in Scotland but still legal in England and Wales. However, the amount specified must be a genuine addition.

Special hazards

If your work involves special hazards or heavy physical or mental strain, and you are a night worker, then you cannot work more than eight hours in any 24. This is not an average but an absolute limit. In other words as soon as you have worked eight hours then you must stop.

5

Pay and Conditions

Payment for work is one of the most contentious areas of employment and it is necessary for any employee to have at least a basic knowledge of their overall entitlement.

Remuneration

A number of legislative provisions exist, affecting remuneration to employees and the way it is paid: the 1970 Equal Pay Act; The Wages Act 1986, consolidated by the 1996 Employment Rights Act and the National Minimum Wage Act 1998. In addition, the 2002 Employment Act has introduced changes to rights of parents and their remuneration. See below.

A recent Act which affects equal pay is the Equality Act 2010. Under this Act it is unlawful for an employer to discriminate against a person because of their sex. This is wide ranging and covers everything from recruitment, employment terms and conditions, pay and benefits, training, promotion, redundancy and dismissal. For the purposes of this chapter, where men and women, working for the same employer, are doing one of the following they are entitled to the same terms in their employment contract:

- The same or similar work
- Work rated as equivalent in a job evaluation study by the employer
- Work of equal value. Pay secrecy clauses in a contract are unenforceable, if an employee or other is trying to find out if any difference in pay is connected with a protected characteristic, for example, sex.

The scope of the various Acts is wide. By S8 of the 1996 Act every employee who works eight hours or more a week has the right to an itemised pay statement. It must state the gross and net amount of pay and the amounts deducted and the purpose of the deduction.

The 1970 Equal pay Act provides that all employees doing the same job be paid equal wages or salary. However, surprisingly, the Act does not include a right for an applicant to serve a questionnaire upon its employer in order to elicit information as to whether or not they are receiving equal pay. There is now a provision in the amended Equal Pay Act 1970 which will allow applicants to issue questionnaires in the same way as they can in race or sex discrimination cases. Whilst employers will not be obliged to answer the questionnaire, a Tribunal hearing the case is entitled to draw adverse inferences from a failure to answer where answers are evasive or equivocal.

The 1986 Wages Act, now consolidated by the 1996 Act defined wages in very broad terms. Wages means 'any sum payable to a worker by his employer in connection with his employment and includes any fee, bonus commission, holiday pay or other emolument referable to his employment, whether payable under his contract or otherwise...' However, a number of payments are specifically excluded and these include expenses and redundancy payments.

One of the effects of the 1986 Wages Act was to abolish the requirement that workers be paid in 'coin of the realm'. We now have the concept of cash-less pay. The 1996 Act only allows deductions from wages if made by virtue of a statutory provision or by a provision of the workers contract, or if the work has previously indicated his agreement in writing to it. There are much stricter controls on retail workers who are defined as being workers who carry out retail transactions directly with members of the public or with fellow workers. Under the Act any deductions in respect of cash shortages or stock deficiencies must not exceed one tenth of the gross amount of wages payable on that day. Also, any sum demanded of such a worker in respect of these losses shall not exceed the 10% figure.

Guarantee payments

Unless a contract of employment expressly or implicitly allows for it, an employee who is laid off is entitled to be paid during the period of such lay off.

To be eligible to receive such a payment, an employee must:

a) have been continuously employed for at least one month when the lay off occurs;
b) have been laid off for the whole of his working hours on a day he is normally required to work;
c) not have unreasonably refused an offer of alternative employment, which was suitable in all the circumstances;
d) have complied with any reasonable requirements imposed by the employer with a view to ensuring that his services are available;
e) not have been laid off because of a strike, lock out or other industrial action involving any employee of the employer or of any associated employer; and
f) have been available for employment on that day.

An employee who is entitled to a guarantee payment is entitled to be paid at the guaranteed hourly rate, subject to a maximum limit for one day. There is a maximum entitlement of five guarantee payments in any period of three months.

Suspension from work on medical grounds

The legislation governing suspension from work on medical grounds was ss 19-22 of the 1978 Act as amended by the Employment Act 1982 consolidated by the Employment Rights Act 1996 and s 64 now deals).

The above Act provides that an employee who is suspended from work is entitled to be paid by his employer if that suspension is in consequence of a requirement imposed under certain statutory provisions or a recommendation made in a Code of Practice issued or approved under s 16 of the Health and Safety at Work Act 1974. There are certain eligibility criteria concerning length of employment etc. An employee is entitled to be paid for up to twenty-six weeks of such suspension after one month's employment.

Provisions relating to sick pay

An employer may have an obligation by virtue of a term in the contract of employment to pay sick pay to employees. Such an obligation may arise as a result of an express term or an obligation may arise under an implied term. The principles governing the implication of terms relating to sick pay were discussed by the court of appeal in Mears v Safecar Security Ltd (1982) where it was held that there is no general presumption of an implied right to sick pay.

Since April 1983 all employers have had a statutory obligation under the Social Security and Housing Benefits Act 1982 to pay Statutory Sick Pay to their employees. The employer pays the employee his statutory sick pay and, until recently then recouped those payments through his National Insurance Contributions.

By the Statutory Sick Pay Act 1994 only those employers who pay less than £2000 in National Insurance contributions can now recoup such payments.

In outline the scheme provides that a qualifying employee is entitled to SSP for the first 28 weeks of sickness (there is no entitlement for the first three days, called 'waiting days') and after that period he will receive state sickness benefit. Certain employees are excluded from the scheme, including pensioners, persons employed for less than three months, persons who do not pay NI contributions and persons who are not employed due to a trade union dispute at their workplace.

More about sick pay

A person may be able to get sick pay if they have been sick for at least four or more days in a row (including weekends, bank holidays and days that you do not normally work). In addition, average weekly earnings were equal to more than the Lower Earnings Limit (LEL). The LEL is the amount a person needs to earn before paying National Insurance Contributions. From 11th April 2012 this was £107 per week. Check for current figures.

From April 2012, you must have average earnings of £107 per week before tax and National Insurance contributions are deducted. Average weekly earnings are calculated over the eight weeks before your sickness began. Only earnings paid in this eight week period can be used for the average weekly earnings.

Agency workers

If agency workers meet the qualifying conditions for payment then it will be payable. It remains payable whilst you are working for your agency. The employer cannot end the contract of service to avoid paying SSP. Whoever is responsible for the deduction of National Insurance contributions from your earnings is also responsible for payment of SSP.

Telling the employer that you are sick and providing evidence

Before the employer can decide on entitlement to SSP, they must be told that you are sick and you must provide evidence. The employer may have their own rules about telling them when you are sick. If they don't, the following will apply:

- The employer should be informed within seven days of the first day that you are sick
- The employer cannot insist that you tell them in person, earlier than the first qualifying day or by a set time, on a special form, on a doctor's statement of fitness for work (fit note) which was previously called a medical certificate or sick note
- More than once a week during your sickness.

The 'fit note' replaced the doctor's sick note on 6th April 2010.

Your employer does not have to pay SSP for any delay in telling them that you are sick. They will pay from the date that they were told as long as you are still sick and the rules for payment are satisfied.

Evidence that you are sick

It is up to your employer to decide whether you are incapable of work for payment of SSP. Your employer cannot ask you to provide medical evidence that you are sick for the first seven days of illness. During this period they may ask you to fill in a self-certificate of their own design or form SC2. If you are sick for more than seven days, your employer can ask you to give them some medical evidence from your doctor. This is used to support payment of SSP.

A 'fit note' from your doctor that says you are not fit for work is strong evidence of sickness. If your employer has strong reasons to believe that you are not sick, they can refuse to pay SSP. They can refuse even if they have strong evidence from your doctor. To help them decide whether or not to pay sick pay, with your consent the employer can get a medical; report from:

- Your doctor
- Their own medical advisors
- A Medical Service Provider through Her Majesty's Revenue and Customs (HMRC).

Maternity and parental pay and leave

Apart from important protection from unfair dismissal because of pregnancy, the Employment Rights Act 1996 provided four further protections in relation to pregnancy - the right to maternity leave, the right to return to work after maternity leave, the right to time off for ante-natal care and the right to maternity pay. The section of the above Act dealing with maternity leave was replaced in its entirety by the Employment Relations Act 1999 Part 1, Schedule 4 which in turn has been amended by the 2002 Employment Act, the provisions of which came into force on April 6th 2003. An amendment was also made by the Maternity and Parental Leave Regulations 2008.

In addition to the above, pregnancy and maternity is now one of the protected characteristics in the Equality Act 2010 and there is now implied into every woman's term of employment a maternity equality clause (s 73 Equality Act 2010). The act protects women from direct discrimination (s 13(1)) and indirect discrimination (s 19(1)) in relation to pregnancy and maternity.

Right to maternity leave

Part V111 of the 1996 Employment Rights Act contains provisions for maternity rights that are further detailed in the Maternity and Parental Leave Regulations 1999. The Directive gives all pregnant employees a general right to maternity leave.

Under the 1999 Employment Rights Act, which came into force on the 15th December 1999, the periods of leave were renamed. Maternity leave became ordinary maternity leave (OML) and additional absence became additional maternity leave (AML).

The regulations now clarify that the term remuneration is now limited to 'sums payable by way of wages or salary'. This means, for example, that women will automatically be entitled to retain a company car and a mobile phone and to receive a performance bonus which is not salary.

All pregnant employees are entitled to 52 weeks maternity leave. This consists of 26 weeks Ordinary Maternity Leave and 26 weeks Additional Maternity Leave. This is available to all employees from the first day of employment. The employee can choose when they start their leave but the earliest it can start is 11 weeks before the baby is due.

The only women not entitled to maternity leave are:

- Share fisherwomen
- Women who normally work abroad (unless they have a work connection with the UK
- Policewomen and women serving in the armed forces

Compulsory maternity leave

An employer may not permit an employee to work during her compulsory maternity period. Compulsory maternity leave is a period of two weeks commencing on the day on which childbirth occurs. An employer who allows a pregnant person to work can be fined.

Giving notice to the employer

In order to qualify for maternity leave the employer must be informed by the end of the 15th week before the baby is due:

- that the employee is pregnant
- the week in which the baby is expected; and
- the date when the employee intends to start ordinary maternity leave.

There is no obligation to put this in writing unless asked to. However, it is a good idea to do so. Once the employer has been informed that maternity leave will be taken they have 28 days to inform you when maternity leave starts.

If the employee has already a contractual right to maternity pay/leave, she may exercise her right to the more favourable terms. If there is a redundancy situation during the leave period and it is not practicable because of the redundancy for the employer to continue to employ her under her existing contract, she is entitled to be offered a suitable vacancy before her employment ends. If a woman intends to return to work before the end of maternity leave, 56 days notice must be given. Since women who qualify now have the right to take Additional Maternity Leave, and there is no obligation to notify the employer during the initial notification, then until notification of a return to work is given, the women will retain the right to return but not pay.

Work during the maternity leave period

Regulation 12A provides that an employee may carry out up to ten days work for her employer during her statutory maternity period (excluding the compulsory maternity period) without bringing her maternity period to an end.

Time off for Ante-natal care

To qualify for this right the employee must have made an appointment for ante-natal care on the advice of a doctor, midwife or health visitor. The employer may not refuse time off for the first visit, but for further appointments, the employer may ask for a certificate or appointment card or other evidence.

Statutory Maternity Pay

The Social Security Act of 1996 and the Statutory Maternity Pay regulations of the same year entitle certain employees to statutory maternity pay. This has been amended by the 2002 Employment Act. SMP is paid for a maximum of 39 weeks. For the first six weeks of maternity leave SMP is paid at 90% of the average gross weekly earnings (before tax and NI) for the remaining 33 weeks it is paid at 90% of gross weekly earnings or £128.73 a week, whichever is the lower.

To claim SMP, a person must tell their employer, 28 days before maternity leave, that they are pregnant and will be off work because of birth. A medical certificate has to be provided.

When is SMP paid?

How long SMP is paid for depends on when the baby is due. It is paid up to 39 weeks. The earliest a person can start maternity leave and start to get SMP is 11 weeks before the baby is due. The latest date to start maternity leave and receiving SMP is the week after the week when the baby is born.

If a person is sick with a pregnancy related illness before the baby is due, SMP will start the week following the week that sickness began. If a person is sick with a non-pregnancy related illness they can claim Statutory Sick pay until the week that the baby is due.

Maternity Allowance

If an employee is not entitled to get SMP they may be entitled to maternity allowance instead.

This is administered through jobcentre plus and a person might get maternity benefit if:

- they are employed, but not eligible for SMP
- they are registered self-employed and paying class C National Insurance Contributions (NIC's) or hold a Small Earnings Exemption Certificate
- they have been very recently employed or self-employed.

Further, they may be eligible if:

- they have been employed or self employed for at least 26 weeks in the 'test period' (66 weeks up to and including the week before the week the baby is due) part weeks count as full weeks; and
- they earned £30 a week averaged over any 13 week period in the test period.

Returning to work after maternity leave

There is an automatic right to return to work after maternity leave and it is assumed the person will do so unless they state otherwise. If a person decides to return earlier than the date notified by the employer, then at least 56 days notice must be given of returning.

Parental leave

The Maternity and Parental Leave Regulations 1999 provide that every person who cares for a young child, or has recently adopted a child, can take time off from work at his or her own convenience to care for that child. Minimum provisions are set for leave, preconditions are set for leave and the notice that an employee has to give an employer before leave can be taken is set out. Employers and employees can agree to vary these provisions by using a workforce agreement as long as it is equal to or more favorable than the statutory provisions.

Any employee who has one year's continuous employment at the date the leave is due to start, and who has, or expects to have, responsibility for a child at that time can apply to take parental leave. A person will have responsibility for a child under the regulations if he/she has parental responsibility under the Children Act 1989 or is registered as the father under the provision of the Births and Deaths Register Act.

Each employee is entitled to take up to 13 weeks of unpaid parental leave in respect of each child born after, or placed for adoption after, 15th December 1999. The right to Parental leave ceases when the child reaches 5 years of age.

Paternity leave

In addition, the 2002 Employment Act widened the scope and range of paternity leave. The Act introduced the right to two weeks paid leave in addition to the 13 weeks unpaid leave. This became effective from April 2003. Leave must be taken within 8 weeks of the birth of the child or placement of the child through adoption.

For employees to claim paternity leave they must:

- Be employed and have worked for their employer for at least 26 weeks before the end of the 15th week before the expected week of childbirth; and
- Be the biological father of the child, or be married to or be the

61

partner of the baby's mother (this includes same sex partners, whether or not they are registered civil partners); and

- Have some responsibility for the child's upbringing; and
- Have given the employer the correct notice to take paternity leave.
- Paternity leave can be taken as a single block of either one or two weeks.

All terms and conditions of employment remain intact during the period of paternity leave except the right to remuneration. Employees are entitled to return to the jobs they had before they took paternity leave.

The Additional Paternity Leave Regulations 2010

The Additional Paternity Leave Regulations 2010 recognise that mothers can often be the main earner for the family and aims to promote shared parenting. The regulations enable eligible employees to have the right to take additional paternity leave and pay. However the right only affects parents of children that are due to be born on or after the 3rd April 2011 or where one or both of the parents have received adoptive notification on or after the 3rd April 2011 that they have been matched with a child for adoption.

Additional Paternity Leave (APL) will allow a father to take up to 26 weeks leave to care for a child and also allows mothers to 'transfer' up to 6 months of maternity leave to their partner. APL will only be able to start 20 weeks after the birth of the child and must end no later then the child's first birthday. In the case of adoption, the earliest APL can start is 20 weeks after the child was placed for adoption and must end no later than one year after the placement began. There is no requirement for the father's leave to begin directly after the mother has returned from statutory maternity Leave or statutory adoption leave and have/or ended their entitlement to statutory maternity or adoption pay, or maternity allowance. In addition, in order to be eligible for Additional Paternity

Leave and Pay (APLP), a father must be continuously employed by the same employer for at least 26 weeks, ending with the relevant week and also remain in the same employment until he starts his leave. In the case of a birth, the relevant week is 15 weeks before the baby is due and in the case of adoption it is the week the adopter is matched with a child for adoption.

Fathers seeking to take APLP must provide a declaration to their employers at least 8 weeks before they wish to start their leave, confirmation of when they intend the leave to start and finish, a declaration stating that they wish to take the leave to care for a child and that the eligibility requirements have been satisfied.

Fathers must also provide a declaration from the mother that provides her employers with her name, address, National Insurance Number and the date she intends to return from maternity leave. The mother must also consent to her employers processing the information and she must confirm that the father has the status he has detailed on his declaration and confirm that he is the only person seeking the leave in respect of the child.

Clearly the new regulations are, to say the least, somewhat complicated and it would be all too easy to fall foul of the required procedures in order to have the potential benefits available. However, the evidence shows that at present many fathers do not use the parental leave that is available to them and it remains to be seen to what extent the Additional Paternity Leave regulations will be used.

Adoption leave and pay

The 2002 Employment Act creates a right for parents to take adoption leave when permanently adopting a child. An adoptive parent is entitled to take 26 weeks paid adoption leave (known as 'ordinary adoption leave') and up to 26 weeks unpaid adoption leave During ordinary adoption leave, employees will be entitled to receive Statutory Adoption Pay (SAP) for 39 weeks of £135.45 per week (2012-2013) or 90% of earnings, whichever is the lower. You should check with the DTI or DSS for current rates.

Qualifying requirements

To be entitled to take adoption leave, employees must have attained 26 weeks service with their employer at the date the adoption takes place. Leave can be taken at any time after the adoption placement begins. Employees will be required to provide evidence of the adoption to the employer. Only one partner in a couple will be able to take adoption leave. The other partner, male or female, will be able to take paternity leave for 2 weeks and receive SPP. There are statutory notice provisions covering how and when employees must inform employers that they wish to take adoption leave. These are flexible and can be verified with the employer.

During the period of ordinary adoption leave the employee is entitled to all their terms and conditions, except the right to remuneration. During the period of additional adoption leave, the employee is in the same position as someone on additional maternity leave – namely that whilst most of the terms and conditions of employment will be suspended, those relating to notice, confidentiality, implied terms of mutual trust and confidence, redundancy terms and disciplinary and grievance procedures will remain in place. The right to return after either ordinary or additional adoption leave mirror's the provisions for ordinary and additional maternity leave respectively.

Insolvency of employer

For the legislation governing the insolvency of an employer, the Employment Rights Act 1996 applies. See also s 175 and schedule 6 of the Insolvency Act 1986. If an employer becomes insolvent an employee acquires certain rights. He becomes a preferential creditor in respect of up to four months-unpaid wages or a maximum set by the Secretary of State. Certain other payments are also deemed to be preferential debts including guarantee payments, payment for time off for trade union activities and payment for ante -natal care.

The employee is entitled to claim payments of certain amounts due to him from his employer from the Secretary of State who will pay them out of the redundancy fund. The classes of debt for which payment may be made include arrears of wages (up to a maximum of 8 weeks) holiday pay (6 weeks) and wages during the statutory minimum notice period.

Statutory right to request a contractual variation-flexible working

The 2002 Employment Act introduced a right to request a contractual variation, where the reason for the request relates to a young child. The 2006 Work and Families Act extended the right, from April 2007 to an employee who cares for, or who expects to care for, an adult. A carer is defined as an employee who is, or expects to be, caring for an adult who is married to, or is the partner or civil partner of the employee or who is a near relative of the employee or falls into neither of these categories but lives at the same address as the employer.

Applications can only be made by parents or potential carers who have worked continuously for an employer for 26 weeks before applying and whose children are under 17 at the time of the application or by parents of disabled children under the age of 18. An employee can request changes to his or her terms and conditions and, in particular, the following:

- Hours of work
- The times when the employee is required to work.
- Where the employee is required to work
- Such other aspects of his or her terms and conditions of employment as the Secretary of State may specify

Procedure for flexible working request

A request for flexible working must:

- State that it is a request for flexible working'
- Specify the changes applied for and the date on which they are to become effective and:
- Explain what effect the changes have on the workplace and how they can propose they can be dealt with

Only one request can be made per year.

Employer's response

The employer must consider the application and can only refuse the application on certain given grounds. These are as follows:

- The burden of additional costs
- The detrimental effect on ability to meet customer demand
- The inability to reorganize work amongst existing staff
- The detrimental impact on quality
- The detrimental impact on performance
- The insufficiency of work during the period the employee proposes to work: and
- Any planned structural changes

Regulations will provide a timetable detailing how the employer must respond to a request for flexible working.

It is likely that an employer will be required to arrange a meeting to consider the request within 28 days of receipt. The employer must give a decision within 14 days of the meeting. If the employee's request is refused, the employer must give grounds for the decision.

An employee will be entitled to appeal but must set out their grounds for appeal. The employer must hear the appeal within 14 days and a decision must be given to the employee within 14 days of the appeal hearing.

Remedies

Where a request has been refused an employee can bring a claim at the Employment Tribunal but only where the employer:

- Has failed to comply with the statutory procedure in considering the application.
- Has refused the request on a ground that is different to the

specified grounds above: or

- Has made the decision based on incorrect facts
- Therefore, there is no jurisdiction for the Employment Tribunal to hear a claim if the employee is merely unhappy about the decision.

If the Tribunal finds against the employer it can:

- Order reconsideration of the issue and/or
- Make an award for compensation

In addition, there will also be the right for employees not to be subjected to a detriment, including dismissal by the employer if they have made an application for flexible working, they have appealed against a refusal to allow flexible working, they have brought proceedings in the Employment Tribunal in respect of a refusal to allow flexible working, or the employee has alleged circumstances which could constitute a ground for bringing such proceedings.

Part Time Workers

There have been significant advances relating to the position of part time workers in relation to remuneration and terms and conditions of employment. The Part-Time Workers (Prevention of Less Favourable Treatment) Regulations 2000 introduced new rights for part time workers. The Part-Time Workers Regulations ensure that Britain's Part Timers are not treated less favourably than comparable full-timers in their terms and conditions, unless it is objectively justified. This means part-timers are entitled to a range of benefits, including:

- The same hourly rates of pay
- The same access to company pension schemes
- The same entitlements to annual leave and maternity/parental leave on a pro-rata basis

- The same entitlement to contractual sick pay
- No less favourable treatment in access to training

Two amendments in 2002 introduced Comparators and occupational pension schemes (regulation 2).

Under the original regulations, part-timers had to compare themselves to full-timers employed under the same type of contract. This meant that, for example a part-timer on a fixed-term contract should compare themselves to a full-timer on a fixed-term contract. This is no longer the case

The other amendment is that of access to occupational pension schemes. Under Regulation 8 (8) of the Part-Time Workers Regulations, where an Employment Tribunal has upheld a complaint from a part-timer for equal access to an occupational pension scheme, the remedies which the tribunal orders may go back no further than two years. In 2001, the House of Lords (Supreme Court) held that this was unlawful in that it contravened European law on the equal treatment of men and women, and could no longer be maintained. As a consequence the law has now been amended to remove the two-year time limit.

Pensions

Pension schemes have become increasingly complex over the years and they have also become notably less generous.

Pensions organised by the employer are called occupational pensions. There are, however, other types of pensions which are not, strictly speaking, occupational pensions. These are generally pensions to which an employer provides a gateway. The state also provides a range of different pensions. In addition, an employee can also save for retirement through personal or stakeholder pensions.

Although there is currently no legal obligation on an employer to set up a pension scheme or to contribute in any way to their employee's pensions, this will change from 2012. The one main requirement will be that all employers with one more employees who do not provide alternative pension arrangements must automatically enrol certain workers into a pension scheme. The employer must make contributions on their workers behalf, register with the Pensions Regulator and provide workers with basic information and how it will affect them. The new employer duties will commence in 2012 and be introduced in stages over six years. Each employer will be allocated a date from when the duties will first apply to them, known as their staging date. For more details of how the changes affect both employer and employee the pensions regulator website www.the pensionsregulator.gov.uk provides more information.

Types of pension

It is a well-known fact nowadays that there is no certainty over the size of the pension that an individual will receive. All you can be sure of is how much has been invested. Personal and stakeholder pensions work on the same basic money purchase principle.

Money purchase schemes

In many ways money purchase schemes are a safer bet than the salary related schemes described further on. This is because every scheme member owns a slice of the pension fund. There is therefore much less that can go wrong. The disadvantage is the lack of certainty about the size of the pension they will provide. This all depends on how much has been put into the scheme and how well the fund has been invested. Charges may be deducted. When you come to claim your pension you purchase an annuity sold by insurance companies and they in return provide a pension.

Salary related schemes

Salary related schemes are the traditional type of occupational pension scheme. These schemes will make a promise as to the amount of pension a person will receive on retirement. The pension will depend on earnings and length of time in the scheme. If investments do badly then it is up to the employer to make up any difference.

69

There are different types of salary related schemes. Some will work out a pension on the basis of a salary when an employee leaves a company, or scheme. Others will work out an average over the total employment. The amounts received and retirement age will vary from scheme to scheme. Some schemes are known as integrated schemes meaning that they claw back some of the occupational pension to take account of what a person receives from the state.

While the theory behind salary related schemes is that the employer bears the risk it does not always work out this way. Employers can go bankrupt and, if a scheme does not have sufficient funds then it may not be able to meet its liabilities. Employers can also say that they want to cut their contributions or no longer wish to carry so much risk. This has become more pronounced within the last few years as stock markets have under-performed.

There are also various hybrid schemes that combine schemes of both types. Employers who provide salary related schemes must also give employees the opportunity to build up extra savings through Additional Voluntary Contributions (AVC's) Employees earning less than £30,000 can take out a stakeholder pension. Like stakeholder pensions AVC's are a money purchase arrangement.

Joining an occupational pension

An employer cannot compel an employee to join an occupational pension scheme. You can also leave a scheme at any time although you may only get a partial refund of contributions if you leave shortly after joining otherwise you will be able to claim the pension accrued on retirement.

Difficulties have arisen by employers excluding certain types of employee from their pension scheme. Pension schemes cannot exclude part timers. However, it is legal for employers to open schemes to staff only after they have been employed for a specific length of time. It is also legal for schemes to give you only one chance to join and if you refuse then to refuse entry in later years.

The law now gives people with disabilities some protection against discrimination. The changes make it harder, although not impossible to exclude employers from the scheme. They can only do this if it can be shown that there is substantial extra risk of an employee taking early retirement.

Leaving a salary related scheme

An employee can leave an employers scheme at any time. This is mostly common on retirement or job change. If you change job what happens depends on how long the period of service is. If it is less than two years then you may get your contributions back minus some tax. Otherwise you will become what is known as a deferred member of the scheme. This means that when you retire you will be paid a pension from the scheme. You also have the right to transfer the pension from your employer's scheme into another pension scheme. You may need professional advice on the wisdom of moving.

When you leave a scheme you should be given a statement of benefits and options within two months. You generally have the right to transfer your pension up until a year before you retire. You can transfer it into your new employers scheme although they don't have to accept it or transfer it into another pension scheme.

If you ask for a transfer value you should be given it within three months.

Rights to information

Members of pension schemes have comprehensive rights to information about their scheme:

- Basic information. This encompasses the broad details of the scheme and should be available on request.

- Annual statements. Members of personal, stakeholder and money purchase occupational schemes should receive annual statements automatically. Members of final salary schemes can request a statement and it should be provided within two months.
- Contributions. If your employer fails for any reason to pay over contributions then the trustees must tell you.
- Early leavers. If you leave a pension scheme before you retire, for example when you change a job, you should be given a statement about your options within two months of leaving.
- Payment of benefits. You should automatically be provided with details of your pension before your retirement date.
- Changes to the scheme. You should automatically be told of any changes to the rules of the scheme.
- You can ask to see any paperwork related to the scheme such as the annual report, trust deed and rules schedule of contributions and the transfer value.

The above outline of pensions is very brief. For further advice refer to the useful addresses section at the back of this book.

6

Terminating Employment

There are a number of ways in which a contract of employment may come to an end-termination by way of contract, termination in breach of contract and termination by methods external to the contract.

At common law, a contract of employment can be validly terminated by an employer giving notice to an employee in accordance with the terms of the contract or, in the absence of such a term, by giving reasonable notice. If sufficient notice was given, the employee had no further rights and this meant that dismissal could be entirely arbitrary. However, in recent times provisions have been introduced whereby an employee may be entitled to compensation for loss of job despite the fact that he was given notice.

It should be noted that once notice has been given, it can only effectively be withdrawn with the consent of the other party.

Dismissal with notice
The length of notice, which must be given by an employer to an employee, is determined by reference to the following criteria to be applied in the following order:

a) Express terms of the contract. If the contract of employment expressly provides for a period of notice, this must be observed unless that period is less than the statutory minimum to which that particular employee is entitled under d) below.

b) In the absence of an express term it may be impossible to imply a term into the contract, for example, by custom. Again, such a period may not be less than the statutory custom.

c) If there is no express or implied term of the contract, the courts may rely on a reasonable period. What is "reasonable" depends upon such factors as the status of the employee, salary, length of employment with that employer, age etc. The "reasonable" period cannot be less than the statutory minimum.

d) Statutory minimum. In the absence of any of the above criteria, or where they produce a period less than the following, the statutory minimum in s 86 of the 1996 Act (ERA) must be applied in respect of those employees covered by that section. Section 86 provides that for an employee continuously employed for between one month and two years, the notice period is one week; for an employee employed for more than two years, he is entitled to one week for each year of continuous employment subject to a maximum of twelve weeks notice after twelve years of employment. These rights do not apply to a contract for the performance of a specific task, which is not expected to last for more than three months.

Constructive dismissal

A constructive dismissal is one where the employee's circumstances become so difficult that they have no option but to leave. This is difficult to prove so a lot of thought must go into a decision to leave in these circumstances.

Summary dismissal

Summary dismissal is where an employer dismisses an employee without giving the employee the amount of notice to which that individual is entitled. If there is no justification, such dismissal is wrongful and an action can be brought.

The remedy for wrongful dismissal is damages representing the loss of wages during the period of notice that ought to have been given. In addition, wrongful dismissal may also be unfair dismissal within the meaning of the 1978 Act.

Circumstances which justify summary dismissal

The question of what justifies summary dismissal is not one that can be answered with a simple rule since each case must be decided according to the particular circumstances. However, a general principle has emerged that summary dismissal is justified if the conduct of the employee is such that it prevents further satisfactory continuance of the relationship. This was the finding in Sinclair v Neighbour (1967).

The status of the employee in question is a relevant consideration as is the fact that the employee has a history of misconduct as opposed to an isolated incident.

Dismissals Procedure

If the contract states that dismissal is to be according to an established pattern (e.g. that there will be two warnings before dismissal occurs) it is a breach of contract if the procedure is not observed. (Tomlinson v L.M.S Rly (1944). If the contract states that the dismissal may only occur for certain specified reasons, a dismissal is wrongful if the reason for the dismissal is other than specified in the contract.

However, it should be noted that the 2002 Employment Act has introduced the obligation on an employer to include a statutory disciplinary and grievance procedure which must be in the contract or written terms and must be followed before any dismissal proceedings can take place.

Waiver of rights

If an employee's conduct justified a summary dismissal, the right must have been exercised within a reasonable time of the conduct, which allegedly justified the action since delay may amount to a waiver of the breach of contract.

Employee leaving

An employee is entitled to terminate employment at any time by giving the amount of notice required by the contract. If the employee is deemed to have been entitled to terminate employment by reason of the employer's conduct that may constitute a constructive dismissal and the fact that he gave notice makes no difference.

If an employer's attitude causes an employee to terminate his contract without notice, this may well constitute constructive dismissal and the employee may act accordingly.

Termination by agreement

The parties to a contract of employment as with any other contract, may terminate their relationship by agreement at any time upon such terms as they may agree, e.g. payment of money as a golden handshake. It should be noted that a termination by agreement is not a dismissal for the purposes of the redundancy and unfair dismissals provisions of the 1996 Act. However, the tribunals are concerned to ensure that any alleged agreement to terminate a contract of employment is real and not merely a result of pressure imposed on an employee who is unaware of the significance of agreeing to terminate the contract and who faces dismissal as an alternative to so agreeing.

Termination by frustration

Frustration occurs whenever the law recognises that without default of either party a contractual obligation has become incapable of being performed because the circumstance in which performance would be called for would render it a thing different from that which was undertaken by the contract (Lord Radcliffe in Davis Contractors v Fareham UDC (1956)).

In the context of a contract of employment, the term frustration means that circumstances have arisen, without the fault of either party, that make it impossible for the contract to be performed in the way that may be reasonably expected and the contract automatically terminates without the need for notice to be given. Frustration of the contract is not deemed to be dismissal for legislative purposes. Examples of frustration may be sickness. In Notcutt v Universal Equipment Co (1986), a worker with 27 years service, who was two years from retirement suffered a permanently incapacitating heart attack. The court decided that this rendered performance of the contract impossible and therefore the contract was frustrated as he was unable to perform his obligation to work. The employee was therefore not entitled to sick pay during his period of notice.

Imprisonment is another example, however this has caused problems. In 1986, the Court of Appeal allowed a four year apprenticeship contract to be frustrated by a six months Borstal sentence: FC Shepherd LTD v Jerrom (1986). In this case court held that such a period of imprisonment made the performance of the contract impossible. As with the sickness, the courts will tend to look at each case on its own merits without applying hard and fast rules.

Action for wrongful dismissal

An employee who has been wrongfully dismissed may bring an action for damages against his former employer representing the amount of wages owed to him in respect of work already done and in respect of wages that the employee would have earned had he been given the amount of notice to which he was entitled. The amount of wages lost is determined by the ordinary principles of common law and includes all sums connected with the job, such as loss of tips etc. Damages for wrongful dismissal cannot normally include compensation for injured feelings or pride or the fact that future earnings may be affected.

The object of damages is to compensate the injured party for what he actually lost, not to punish the party in breach of contract, and therefore the courts have developed principles to ensure that the employee who has been wrongfully dismissed receives compensation only for his actual loss.

Damages against employee

Where an employee fails to give sufficient notice to his employer, the employer may sue the employee for damages representing the loss, which follows from the breach of contract. In practice, such actions are infrequent because the loss is often minimal.

Specific performance

Specific performance is an order from the court directing that the parties to a contract perform their contractual obligations. It is a fundamental principle of labour law that specific performance is granted to compel performance of a contract of employment and this principle is now embodied in s 235 of the Trade Union and Labour Relations (Consolidation) Act 1992.

Injunction

An injunction is an order from a court forbidding certain conduct, e.g. the breaking of a term of the contract of employment. Hence it may be used to prevent a breach of a covenant restraining an employee from taking employment with a rival of his former employer. The courts usually refuse to grant an injunction if it compels performance.

By virtue of the Trade Union and Labour Relations Act 1992, no court may issue an injunction if the effect of such an order would be to compel an employee to do any work or to attend any place to work.

However, where the injunction compelling performance is to the benefit of the employee, the court may be prepared to grant such an order. In Hill v CA Parsons LTD (1972) the defendant employers wished to enter into an agreement with an organisation of workers whereby it was agreed that all employers in certain sections, including the plaintiff, would be obliged to join that organisation. This arrangement was legal at the time but under the Industrial Relations Act 1971 it would have been invalid. The plaintiff did not wish to join the organisation and he was dismissed with four weeks notice. The Court of Appeal held that he was wrongfully dismissed since he was entitled to at least six months notice and furthermore an injunction was awarded which prevented the employee from being dismissed until that time elapsed by which time he would have a remedy under the 1971 Act.

Declaration

A declaration is an order from the court, which simply determines the rights of the parties in the case. It has no binding force in itself and is not available to all employees being restricted to those persons whose employment is derived from statute.

Written statement of reasons for dismissal

An employee who has been continuously employed for at least a year and who has been dismissed, subject to the statutory provisions of the 2002 Act and the following of a formal procedure, is entitled to receive, upon request, a written statement of the reasons for his dismissal. A claim may be presented to an industrial tribunal by an employee that his employer has "unreasonably" refused to provide a written statement of the reasons for dismissal or that it is inadequate or untrue. The right to a written statement only arises where the employee has been dismissed by his employer.

Suspension

In accordance with the general principle that an employer fulfils his contractual obligations by paying wages in accordance with the contract of employment, he may suspend an employee on full wages without breach of contract. An employer may only suspend an employee without pay if the contract expressly or impliedly provided for this. If the contract does not so provide, it is a breach of contract. Therefore, an employee who is suspended without contractual authority may treat himself as dismissed and claim accordingly.

Unfair Dismissal

The present law relating to unfair dismissal is to be found in the

Employment Rights Act 1996. The significance of the concept of unfair dismissal is that it represents a further, and most important, step towards recognising the property right, which an employee has in his job. Additionally, it is no longer possible for an employer to end a contract by simply giving notice and thereby totally discharging his responsibilities. The threat of dismissal is no longer quite so important since the employee has a remedy if the threat is implemented.

The 1996 Act provides that, subject to certain specified exceptions, every employee has the right not to be unfairly dismissed. It should be noted that a complaint of unfair dismissal does not depend upon the employer having acted in breach of contract but simply that the employer has terminated the contract in circumstances which are unfair.

Certain categories of employees are excluded: employees who, at the effective date of termination of the contract have been continuously employed for less than one year, *two years if employed after 6th April 2012*, persons over retiring age, persons employed in the police service, share fishermen, employees who ordinarily work outside Great Britain, employees employed on fixed term contracts and persons covered by a designated dismissals procedure agreement.

Dismissal

If an action for unfair dismissal is to succeed, the employee must first establish that he was dismissed within the meaning of the Act. The employee must establish constructive dismissal if alleged.

The Act provides that:

"an employee shall be treated as dismissed by his employer if the contract under which he is employed by the employer is terminated by the employer whether it is so terminated by notice or without notice or where under that contract he is employed for a fixed term, that term expires without being renewed under the same contract or the employee

80

terminates that contract, with or without notice, in circumstances such that he is entitled to terminate it without notice by reason of the employers conduct".

The Act refers to the concept of so-called "constructive' dismissal. If an employee leaves employment entirely voluntarily, there is no dismissal but if he leaves because of the employers conduct then it may be deemed "constructive"

The courts and tribunals have been concerned to define the circumstances in which an employee is entitled to regard himself as having been constructively dismissed. In Western Excavating LTD v Sharp (1978) the tribunals found that sufficiently unreasonable behaviour on the part of the employer entitled an employee to leave his job and claim constructive dismissal. However, the Court of Appeal rejected the unreasonableness test and established that the correct test is one based on strict contractual principles. Accordingly, an employee is only able successfully to argue constructive dismissal where the employer has breached the contract in such a way as to justify the employee in treating himself as discharged from further performance. The action of an employer may involve breach of an express or implied term.

When is dismissal unfair?

The expression "unfair dismissal" is in no sense a commonsense expression capable of being understood by the person in the street. Whether a dismissal is unfair is affected, but not conclusively determined, by whether one or both parties has broken the terms of the contract of employment. The employer cannot, in seeking to show that a dismissal was not unfair rely on alleged misconduct not known to him at the time of the dismissal. An otherwise fair dismissal is not automatically rendered unfair by a failure to give proper notice.

Reasonableness. It is for the employer to establish the reason for the dismissal. The tribunal must then satisfy itself as to whether the employer acted reasonably or unreasonably. The EAT laid down the following general principles in Iceland Frozen Foods v Jones (1982):

a) In applying the provisions of the 1996 Act a tribunal must consider the reasonableness of the employers conduct and not simply whether they (the members of the tribunal) consider the dismissal unfair.

b) In judging the reasonableness of the employer's conduct a tribunal must not substitute its own decision as to what was the right course to adopt for that of the employer.

c) In many cases there is a band of reasonable responses to the employees conduct within which one employer might take one view and another quite reasonably another.

d) The function of the tribunal is to determine whether in the particular circumstances the decision to dismiss fell within the band of reasonable responses, which a reasonable employer might have adopted. If the dismissal falls within the band it is fair. If it falls outside the band it is unfair.

In deciding whether an employer acted reasonably, the industrial tribunal is required to have regard to the provisions of the ACAS Code of Practice-Disciplinary Code of Practice and Procedures in Employment. In broad terms, this provides that the disciplinary rules and procedures ought to have been made known to each employee and that a disciplinary procedure ought to contain certain essential procedures.

Reasons for dismissal

There are five categories of reasons, which, if one is established by the employer, may make the dismissal fair provided that the tribunal is satisfied that the employer acted reasonably.

These are as follows:
a) Capability or qualification
b) Conduct
c) Redundancy
d) Illegality of continued employment
e) Some other substantial reason.

In addition, an employer in certain circumstances, can dismiss an employee for reasons connected to pregnancy. Usually, it is automatically unfair to do so unless the employer can establish that at the effective date of termination, because of her pregnancy, she:

a) is or will have become incapable of adequately doing the work she is employed to do or: or
b) cannot or will not be able to do the work she is employed to do without a contravention (either by her or her employer) of a duty of restriction imposed by law.

In Brown v Stockton on Tees Borough Council (1988) the House of Lords (Supreme Court) held that if a woman was selected for redundancy because she is pregnant, such a dismissal is automatically unfair. Indeed, Lord Griffith stated that "it surely cannot have been intended that an employer should be entitled to take advantage of a redundancy situation to weed out his pregnant employer".

However, even where the circumstances of a and b above apply, the dismissal is still unfair if the employer has a suitable vacancy, i.e. appropriate for a pregnant woman to do and not substantially less favourable than her existing employment in relation to the nature, terms and place of employment, which he fails to offer her.

Dismissal for trade union reasons
References in this section are to the Trade Union and Labour Relations

(Consolidation) Act 1992. Trade Union membership or activities. Except in exceptional cases, a dismissal is automatically unfair if the employee can establish that the principal reason for it was that the employer was, or proposed to become, a member of an independent trade union, or that the employee had taken or proposed to take part in the activities of an independent trade union at any appropriate time or that the employee was not a member of any or a particular trade union, or had refused or proposed to refuse to become or remain a member.

Other reasons for dismissal

An industrial tribunal cannot determine whether a dismissal was fair or unfair if it is known that at the date of dismissal the employer was conducting or instituting a lock out or the complainant was taking part in a strike or other industrial action, unless it is shown:

a) that one or more relevant employees of the same employer have not been dismissed: or
b) that any such employee has, before the expiry of the period of three months beginning with the employee's date of dismissal, been offered re-engagement and that the complainant has not been offered re-engagement.

National security

If an employee has shown to have been dismissed on grounds of national security, as evidenced by a certificate signed by or on behalf of a minister of the Crown, the tribunal must dismiss the complaint.

In Council of Civil Service Unions v Minister for the Civil Service (1985) (the GCHQ case), the court held that the requirements of national security outweighed those of fairness when the minister decided to ban trade unions at GCHQ, without consultation with the trade unions. Workers who refused to give up their trade union membership were subsequently fairly dismissed.

Procedure

An employee who considers that he has been unfairly dismissed may present a complaint to the Central Office of Industrial Tribunals within three months of the effective date of termination or within such further period as the tribunal considers reasonable in a case where it is satisfied that it was not reasonably practicable for the complaint to be presented within a time period of three months.

Where the dismissal is unfair (failure to offer re-engagement where the dismissal is connected with a lockout or strike) the time limit is six months from the date of dismissal.

A copy of the application is sent to the employer as respondent. If the employer wishes to contest any aspect of the complaint, he must enter a "notice of appearance" within 14 days, although tribunals have a wide discretion to grant an extension of time. Once this has happened, a date is set down for the hearing of the case by an industrial tribunal.

Conciliation

A copy of the application is also sent to a conciliation officer. He is under a statutory duty, either at the request of the parties or on his own initiative, to endeavor to promote a voluntary settlement of the issue, either by way of an agreement to reinstate or re-engage the complainant or an agreement as to the payment of compensation in respect of the dismissal. there is no legal duty upon the parties to co-operate with the conciliation officer.

Pre-hearing Assessments

Under the Industrial Tribunals Regulations (S1 1985/16) provision is made for a pre-hearing assessment of the case to be made at the request of either of the parties or on the notion of the tribunal itself. At the tribunal, it is for the complainant to establish that he was dismissed (unless dismissal is conceded). It is then for the tribunal to satisfy itself as to whether the dismissal was fair or unfair in accordance with the principles stated above.

If the dismissal is found to be unfair, the tribunal will consider the remedies, which may be awarded. An appeal, on a point of law only, lies from an industrial tribunal to the Employment Appeal Tribunal.

Remedies

Reinstatement and re-engagement orders. If the Tribunal finds the dismissal unfair, it must explain to the complainant the remedies available and ask if he wishes to be reinstated or re-engaged. If the employee indicates that this is his wish then the Tribunal must consider whether it is practicable for the employer to comply with such an order. If the employer complies, but not fully, with a reinstatement or re-engagement order then, unless the tribunal is satisfied that it was not practicable to comply with the order, an additional award of compensation must be made.

If a reinstatement or re-engagement order is made but not complied with at all or if no such order is made, the tribunal must make an award of compensation on the basis of the following:

a) basic award, amount of which is calculated in line with redundancy payments;
b) compensatory award, being an amount that the tribunal considers just and equitable in all the circumstances having regard to the loss suffered by the complainant in consequence of the dismissal in so far as the loss is attributable to action taken by the employer subject to a maximum limit.

7

Discrimination in the Workplace

The ability of employers to discriminate in the workplace has been steadily eroded. In 2010, the Equality Act came onto the statute books and was implemented in two stages, October 2010 and April 2011. The Act replaced nine previous pieces of legislation, bringing them all under one umbrella.

The main changes contained within the Equality Act 2010 are making pay secrecy gagging clauses unenforceable, putting restrictions on employers asking job applicants questions about disability or health, making employers responsible for protecting their staff from harassment by customers and allowing employment tribunals that find an employer has discriminated against an employee to make recommendations that could affect the whole workforce.

The Equality Act replaced the Equal Pay Act 1970, The Sex Discrimination Act 1975, the Race Relations Act 1976, The Disability Discrimination Act 1996, The Employment Equality (Sexual Orientation) Regulations 2003, The Employment equality (Religion or Belief) Regulations 2003 and the Employment Equality (Age) Regulations 2006, the Equality Act 2006 and the Equality Act (Sexual Orientation) Regulations 2007. In most cases, the thrust of the Acts that were incorporated into the Equality Act 2010 have remained unchanged, but are now contained within the new legislation. Outlined below are the main points of the Acts.

Equal Pay

In broad terms, the Equal Pay Act 1970, which has now been replaced wholesale by the Equality Act 2010, was concerned with less favourable treatment of one person relative to another in respect of matters governed by the contract under which a person is employed whereas the Sex Discrimination act 1975 dealt with less favourable treatment in matters not governed by the contract, on grounds of sex and/or marital status.

The Equal Pay Act 1970 was influenced by the treaty of Rome and the effect of certain European Community Directives have been considerable in this area and have significant practical consequences for any applicant contemplating bringing an action alleging breach of the Equality Act 2010.

Article 119 of the Treaty of Rome provides that: "each member state shall maintain the application of the principle that men and women should receive equal pay for equal work. For the purpose of this article, pay means the ordinary basic or minimum wage or salary and any other consideration, whether in cash or kind, which the worker receives, directly or indirectly in respect of his employment from his employer. The Article is directly enforceable by individuals in the courts of member states of the EEC. The 2002 Employment Rights Act introduced the right of the employee to give the employer a questionnaire in order to ascertain whether or not the employer is actually paying and treating equally. The employer does not have to comply.

Sex Discrimination Act 1975

This Act has also been replaced wholesale by the Equality Act 2010. In relation to employment, the Sex Discrimination Act was intended to render discrimination on the grounds of sex and/or the fact that a person is married unlawful as regards those areas of employment not dealt with by the terms of the contract. The Act rendered discrimination on the above grounds unlawful except in the following cases.

a) Discrimination by way of special treatment afforded to women in connection with pregnancy or childbirth.

b) Where in the previous year there were no or few members of one sex doing a particular job, certain discrimination in favour of members of that sex is allowed.

c) Discrimination in the selection, promotion or training of a person is permissible where being a man or woman is a genuine occupational qualification.

d) There are special rules relating to the police, prison officers and ministers of religion.

e) There are special rules relating to death or retirement. The position here had been much influenced by community law which in turn led to the amendment of the Sex Discrimination Act 1986. Under Community law it is quite clear that the domestic legislation of a member state may fix discriminatory retirement ages.

Section 6 of the Act provided that the following areas of employment are within the scope of the act.

a) Arrangements for selecting of employees and making offers of employment.

b) The terms upon which employment is offered but not the terms themselves when employment has been obtained, this latter matter being within the scope of the Equality Act 2010.

c) Access to promotion, training, transfer or any other benefit, facilities or services.

d) Dismissal or the subjecting of a person to any other detriment, e.g., suspension from work.

It is unlawful to publish, or cause to be published an advertisement which indicates, or might reasonably indicate, an intention to do an act which was contrary to the Act.

The meaning of discrimination. The Act embodied three kinds of discrimination, direct discrimination unfavourable treatment on grounds of race, sex etc. Indirect discrimination-this is where the complainant must demonstrate that the employer applies a requirement or condition which he applies or would apply to members of the other sex/single persons. That it is to the complainants detriment because he or she cannot comply with it.

An example of the operation of this provision would be where an employer requires all his employees to be over six feet tall. This could only be justified if the employer could demonstrate that the job demanded it.

One important case in this area is Price v Civil Service Commission (1978) Held: a civil service condition that candidates for certain posts should be no more than 28 years of age was indirect discrimination because women in their late twenties were frequently occupied in having and rearing children.

Discrimination by victimisation. S 4, this dealt with discrimination against a person who has brought proceedings, given evidence, information, alleged a contravention etc under the Sex Discrimination Act or Equal Pay Act. Such a person must not be treated less favourably by the alleged discriminator than another person in those circumstances was or would be treated.

In relation to discrimination on grounds of sex (as opposed to discrimination against married persons) s7 provides that certain kinds of employment are excluded from the operation of the Act, namely where being a member of one sex is a "genuine occupational qualification" for the job. Two general points should be noted:

a) These provisions do not apply to the terms upon which employment is offered, dismissal or subjecting a person to any other detriment.

b) These provisions do not apply to the filling of a vacancy where the employer already has male (or female) employees capable of filling it and whom it would be reasonable to employ on those duties and whose numbers are sufficient to meet the employer's likely requirements without undue inconvenience.

Being a man or woman is a genuine occupational qualification for a job where the essential nature of the job calls for a man for reasons of physiology or authenticity e.g. actors, models etc. In addition where the job needs to be held by a man to preserve decency or privacy or the job is likely to involve the holder doing work or living in a private home and needs to be held by a same sex person because objections might be raised to a member of the opposite sex in attendance. Also, the nature or the location of the establishment effectively requires the employee to live in and in the absence of separate sleeping accommodation and sanitary facilities, it is not reasonable to expect the employer to provide such things. In addition, the nature of the establishment where the work is done, i.e. a hospital or prison requires that the job be done by a man.

Sexual Orientation

The Court of Appeal in R v Ministry of Defence Ex p Smith (1996) stated that sex discrimination legislation was aimed at gender discrimination not orientation discrimination. However, from December 2003 the position became clearer with the introduction of the Employment Equality (Sexual Orientation) Regulations 2003 (now replaced by the Equality Act 2010), which gave effect to the EU Directive on discrimination and which makes both direct and indirect discrimination on the grounds of sexual orientation unlawful. The law concerning transsexuals, those who have undergone or intend to undergo gender realignment has also been covered by legislation, the relevant legislation being The Sex Discrimination (Gender Reassignment) Regulations 1999 (Now replaced by the Equality Act 2010) which amended the Sex Discrimination Act to specifically include discrimination on the grounds of gender reassignment.

Race Relations Act 1976

The 1976 Act, now replaced in full by the Equality Act 2010, was concerned with discrimination on grounds of colour, race, nationality, or ethnic or national origin. Some difficulty has been experienced over the question of the meaning of ethnic origin and in particular its relationship with race.

An important defining case in this respect was Mandla v Lee (1983). The House of Lords resolved the matter. The question was whether Sikhs are a group of persons defined by ethnic origin so as to fall within the protection of the Act. It was held that Sikhs did constitute an ethnic group. "Ethnic" was used in the Act in a sense much wider than that of "race" and an ethnic group can be identified by some or all of such essential factors as a long history, cultural tradition, common geographical origin, common language and a common religion.

It should be noted that a racial group cannot be defined by the factor of language alone.

The 1976 Act was concerned not only with employment but covers such things as the provision of services, housing etc. There are a number of exceptions to the 1976 Act including where being of a certain race etc is deemed to be a genuine occupational qualification, such as specific providers of services to defined communities.

Discrimination on the grounds of disability

In 1995 the Disability Discrimination Act was passed. This has now been replaced wholesale with the 2010 Equality Act. In relation to employment, it made all employers of over 20 employees or more legally liable for discrimination against disabled people. Part 11 of the Act, relating to employment, came into force at the end of 1996 at which time a code of practice came into in force to help on interpretation. To be protected against discrimination an individual must be a person who has a disability or had a disability. Disability is defined as physical or mental impairment, which has a substantial and long-term effect on the person's ability to carry out day-to-day activities.

In relation to employment the individual is protected against discrimination. It should be noted that the Act only mentioned discrimination on the grounds of disability and thus, unlike the Race Relations Act and Sex Discrimination Act allowed an employer to positively discriminate in the case of a person with a disability.

The Act, in s 4 outlines acts of discrimination. These principally cover the arrangements for appointing employees, the terms on which employment is offered and refusal of employment. It is also unlawful to discriminate in the terms of employment, in the opportunities offered for training, promotion, transfer or any other benefit or to dismiss a person because of disability.

Age discrimination in the workplace

On 1ˢᵗ October 2006, The Employment Equality (Age) Regulations (EE(A) Regs) took effect, outlawing age discrimination in both the workplace and vocational training. These Regulations have now been replaced wholesale by the Equality Act 2010. It is against the law to treat a person unfairly at work because of age. It is against the law to discriminate for being too young or old. The law only covers work, adult education and training. The law applies to a person whether working or applying for a job. It is against the law to bully or make offensive comments in the workplace because of age.

There are some exceptions to the general rule. For example, an employer may occasionally be allowed to discriminate against someone because of their age but only if they can show that this is justified. An employer may argue that it doesn't make business sense to employ someone over 60 years of age if there is a long and involved period of training allied to the job.

Retirement and age discrimination

The normal retirement age for both men and women is 65, unless the employment contract states that it is higher. An employer was allowed to force a person to retire at the normal retirement age. However, with the scrapping of the Default Retirement Age between April and October 2011, employers will no longer be able to force employees to retire at 65.

Job applications and discrimination

It is generally against the law for employers to refuse to take a person on or promote because of age. In most cases employers shouldn't target adverts at specific age groups. There are some exceptions to this rule.

Unfair dismissal

It is discriminatory to dismiss a person because of age. A claim for unfair dismissal may be made if this has been the case.

8

Being Made Redundant

Compensation for redundancy was one of the first employment protection rights introduced into our law. The first piece of legislation was the Redundancy Payments Act 1965 and the law is now contained in the main in the Employment Rights Act 1996 s 139. In addition, the Equality Act 2010 now has a bearing (see below).

In order to claim a redundancy payment an employee must have two years continuous service and be dismissed for reasons of redundancy. The definition of dismissal for redundancy purposes is contained within s 136 of the Employment Rights Act 1996.

These situations are the same as unfair dismissal that is, employer termination with or without notice, a fixed term contract expiring and constructive dismissal In addition, by s 139(4), if the employment is terminated by the death, dissolution or liquidation of the employer, or the appointment of a receiver, there is dismissal for reasons of redundancy.

The definition of redundancy is found in s 139(1) of the Act. This states that a redundancy has occurred if the dismissal is wholly or mainly attributable to:

a) the fact that his employer has ceased or intends to cease, to carry on the business for the purposes for which the employee was employed by him, or has ceased, or intends to cease, to carry on that business in the place where the employee was so employed or...

b) the fact that the requirements of that business for employees to carry out work of a particular kind, or for employees to carry out work of a particular kind in the place where he was so employed, have ceased or diminished or are expected to cease or diminish. This means that the redundancy occurs in three situations - the employer increasing business the employee moving his place of business or the employer reducing his labour force.

One key case dealing with redundancy was that of Murray v Foyle Meats Ltd (1999) IRLR 562. The House of Lords (Supreme Court) held that the definition of redundancy requires two factual questions to be answered. These are: have the requirements of the employer's business for employees to carry out work of a particular kind ceased or diminished, or were they expected to cease or diminish? Was the dismissal of the employee attributable, wholly or mainly, to this state of affairs? This means looking at the employer's overall requirements to decide whether there has been a reduced need for employees irrespective of the terms of the individual's contract or of the function that each performed.

Consultation

If an employer employs 20 employees or less then it is an individual consultation. If more than 20 employees are involved then this is a collective redundancy and a 90-day consultation period is required.

An important requirement in redundancy situations is the need for consultation. Consultation may be directly with the employees concerned or with their representatives. It should be observed that while the size of an undertaking might affect the nature or formality of the consultation, it cannot excuse lack of consultation at all.

Failure to consult the employee about his redundancy may render the dismissal unfair. Unions must be consulted too. Where the employer has broken his statutory duty to consult, the union or employee representatives can apply to a tribunal for a protective award which is payable to those employees in respect of whom the representatives should have been consulted. Similar provisions relate to consultation where there is a transfer of an undertaking under the Transfer of Undertakings Regulations 1981. Where such a transfer takes place, Regulation 10 creates a duty on both the transferor and the transferee to inform the representatives. The remedy for failure to comply with the consultation provisions under the regulations is found in Regulation 11. The employer can raise the defence of special; circumstances. The maximum award which can be made under the Regulations is four weeks pay. This is set off against any protective award given to the employee. Since 1993, the duty on the tribunal to offset this payment against wages or payment in lieu of notice is removed.

A key case dealing with consultation and redundancy is that of Mugford v Midland Bank plc (1977) IRLR 208. In this case, the EAT held that a dismissal on the grounds of redundancy was not unfair because no consultation had taken place with the employee individually, only the recognized trade union. The EAT described the position with regard to consultation as follows: where no consultation about redundancy has taken place with either the trade union or the employee, the dismissal will normally be unfair, unless the reasonable employer would have concluded that the consultation would be an utterly futile exercise; consultation with the trade union over the selection criteria does not of itself release the employer from considering with the employee individually his or her being identified for redundancy; it will be a question of fact and degree for a tribunal to consider whether the consultation with the individual and/or the trade union was so inadequate as to render the dismissal unfair.

According to King v Eaton Ltd (1996) consultation must be fair and proper, which means that there must be:

- Consultation when the proposals are still at a formative stage
- Adequate information and adequate time to respond
- A conscientious consideration by the employer of the response to consultation.

Consultation about collective redundancies
The provisions of the European Council Directive 98/59/EC on the approximation of the laws of Member states relating to collective

redundancies (the Collective Redundancies Directive) are now contained in Pt 1V, Ch 11 TULCRA which outlines the procedure for handling collective redundancies. For these purposes, s 195(1) TULCRA defines a redundancy dismissal as 'for a reason not related to the individual concerned or for a number of reasons all of which are not so related'.

The consultation should be about ways of avoiding the dismissals, reducing the number of employees to be dismissed, and mitigating the circumstances of the dismissals. It is necessary for the employer to consult on each of these three aspects and not just on some of them. There is an obligation for the employer to undertake such consultations with a view to reaching agreement with the appropriate representatives. The employer must disclose the following information in writing to these representatives:

1. The reason for the proposal;
2. The numbers and descriptions of employees whom it is proposed to dismiss;
3. The total number of employees of any description employed by the employer at the establishment;
4. The proposed method of selecting those to be dismissed;
5. The proposed method of calculating payments if different from those required by statute; and
6. The number of agency works working temporarily for and under the supervision and direction of the employer; the parts of the employers undertaking in which they are engaged and the types of work they are carrying out.

Special circumstances

There are two 'escape' clauses for employers unable to comply with their obligations under s 188 TULCRA 1992:

1. Where there are special circumstances which make it not reasonably practicable for an employer to comply with the

consultation and information requirements they are to take all steps towards compliance that are reasonably practicable in the circumstances;

2. Where they have invited affected employees to elect representatives and the employees have failed to do so within a reasonable time, then the employer must give all the affected employees the information set out above.

One key case outlining special circumstances is that of the Bakers Union v Clarke of Hove Ltd (1978) IRLR 366. The court held that there were three stages to deciding whether there was a defence in any particular case. First, were there special circumstances? Second, did they render compliance with the statute not reasonably practicable? Third, did the employer take all the reasonable steps towards compliance as were reasonably practicable in the circumstances? In this case, insolvency was not special enough in itself to provide a defence.

Special circumstances mean something out of the ordinary or something that is not common. In any complaint to the Employment Tribunal the onus is on the employer to show that there were special circumstances.

Misconduct and redundancy

Section 140(1) of the Employment Rights Act 1996 provides that in certain situations the employee will be disentitled to a redundancy payment. This occurs when the employee terminates the contract where:

a) the employee commits an act of misconduct and the employer dismisses without notice or

b) the employee commits an act of misconduct and the employer dismisses with shorter notice than the redundancy notice or

(c) the employer, when the redundancy notice expires, gives the employee a statement in writing that the employer is entitled, by virtue of the employee's conduct, to dismiss without notice.

There are two exceptions to this. By s 140 (2) where an employee, while under notice of redundancy, takes part in a strike or other industrial action to protest against the redundancies. If however, an employee who is on strike is selected for redundancy, the tribunal will have no jurisdiction to hear the case unless there are selective dismissals (Simmons v Hoover (1977)).

By S 143 the employer can extend the redundancy notice period and require the employees to work in order to make up the days lost by the industrial action and if the employees lose they disentitle themselves to a redundancy payment.

Suitable alternative employment

If the employer offers the employee his old job back or a different job which is suitable alternative employment, the new contact starts on the termination of the old or within four weeks of the old contract expiring and the employee unreasonably refuses the offer he is disentitled to a redundancy payment by virtue of sections 141(2) and (3). The section therefore means that two questions must be asked: is the offer suitable alternative employment and is the employee's refusal of that offer reasonable.

Trial period in new employment

If the terms of the new contract differ (wholly or in part) from the old contract, then by s 138 the employee is entitled to a trial period. By subsection (3) the statutory trial period is four weeks, but this can be extended by the employees contract as long as the period is in writing and specified precisely. If the employee is dismissed during the trial period, he is treated as being dismissed for the reason his original contract ended, that is, redundancy, and on the date his original contract ended, so entitling him to claim a redundancy payment. If the employee resigns, he is treated as dismissed for redundancy, unless his resignation was unreasonable.

Lay off and Short time working

In order to prevent redundancies, the employer may temporarily lay off his workers to put them on short time. By s 147 a lay off is where no work or pay is provided by the employer. Short time working is where less than half a weeks pay is earned. By s 148 where the lay off or short time has lasted for more than four consecutive weeks or six weeks in any thirteen, the employee can give notice to his employer that he intends to claim a redundancy payment. He must give the notice in writing. The employer has a defense if he can show that he reasonably expects to provide full time work for the next thirteen weeks and he raises this defense in written counter notice served within seven days of receipt of the employee's intention to claim.

Redundancy compensation

A redundancy payment is calculated in the same way as the basic award for unfair dismissal and is therefore based on age and years of service. However, unlike the basic award, periods of employment below the age of 18 do not count and the employees period of continuity is deemed to start at his 18th birthday. (Employment Rights Act 1996 s 211(2)). Again, unlike the basic award there is no deduction for contributory conduct, but like the basic award, there will be no reduction for each month the employee works in the year before he attains the normal retirement age for the job, so that on reaching the age, or 65, whichever is lower, entitlement to a redundancy payment ceases.

If the redundancy is caused by the employer's insolvency, the employee may make a claim for a redundancy payment to the Department of Employment under s 166 of the Employment Rights Act 1996. While the Employee ranks as a preferential creditor in his employer's insolvency, this will not be much use if the employer has no assets and therefore additionally the Department can pay certain sums to the employee from the National Insurance Fund. This can be up to eight weeks wages, up to six weeks holiday pay, a basic award and other payments.

What is paid?

- For each complete year of employment after an employee's forty first birthday there is an entitlement to one and a half week's pay
- For each complete year of employment after an employees twenty second birthday but before turning forty one there is an entitlement to one weeks pay
- For each complete year of employment whilst either 18, 19, 20 or 21 the entitlement is a half week's pay.

There is a ceiling of 20 years worth of redundancy pay.

Transfers of Undertakings

The Transfer of Undertakings (Protection of Employment Regulations)) (TUPE) 2006 completely replaced the 1981 TUPE Regulations governing transfer of employment from one employer to another when a company/organization is merged/sold with or to another.

A transfer of undertaking is defined, in TUPE 2006 reg. 3(1) as being 'the transfer of an economic entity which retains its identity'. Reg 3.(2) goes on to define an economic entity. Regulation 4 provides that, on transfer the contracts of employment of employees of the transferor are automatically transferred to the transferee. The transferee takes over all the rights and liabilities of the contracts of employment except for the occupational pension scheme (reg 10). There is another important provision in regulation 7 which states that dismissal of an employee either before or after a transfer will be automatically unfair if sole or principal reason for the dismissal is either the transfer itself or a reason connected with the transfer which is not an economic, technical or organizational reason entailing changes in the workforce.

Redundancy and the Equality Act 2010

The Equality Act 2010 now affects all areas of work, including redundancy. An employer cannot select a person for redundancy just because they are disabled. The criteria used to select people for redundancy must not put disabled people at a disadvantage unless there is a fair and balanced reason for doing this. The employer must make reasonable adjustments to any criteria used to select employees for redundancies. For more information on the Equality Act 2010 you should go to the Equality and Human Rights Commission website www.equalityhumanrights.com.

9

Health and Safety at Work

The Health and Safety at Work Act 1974.

Although not seen as implied duties in the contract of employment, it would be incomplete to talk about the employer's liability in relation to the safety of his employees without a brief overview of the statutory provisions.

The 1974 Act was introduced as a result of the Robens Committee report of 1972. The Committee found that the law on health and safety was piecemeal and badly structured, with eleven pieces of major legislation supplemented by over 500 supplementary statutory provisions. The majority of the law based liability on occupation of premises. The Committee proposed a unification of the law, basing liability on employment not occupation of premises.

The Committees findings were embodied in the Health and Safety at Work Act 1974. The aim of the Act is twofold - to lay down general duties across the whole area of employment, and to provide a unified system of enforcement under the control of the Health and Safety Executive and local authorities. General duties are imposed upon various types of people, for example employers, suppliers and manufacturers, with the aim of ensuring a safe working environment.

Section 2(1) lays down the general duty on employers: "It shall be the duty of every employer to ensure, so far as is reasonably practicable, the health, safety and welfare of all his employees. This is further specified by subsection (2). The phrase to which all these duties are subject is "so far as is reasonably practicable". The basis of the duties under s 2(2) is that of employment - it covers duties owed by n employer to his employees; the duties, however, extend beyond the employment relationship. Section 3(1) provides that employers should conduct their business in such a way, "in so far as is reasonably practicable to protect persons other than their own employees from risks to their health and safety.

Liability is imposed not only on those who physically occupy premises but also on those who are responsible for the maintenance of such premises, or the access to and exit from the premises. In addition, liability is imposed against those responsible for safety and absence of risk concerning plant or substances used on the premises.

Protection of those other than employees is continued in s 5. This imposes a duty on those who control work premises to use the best means practicable to prevent the emission of offensive or noxious substances and to render harmless any such substances, which are so emitted. This general duty overlaps with the more specific duties laid down in the Control of Pollution Act 1974.

The Act attempts to increase protection by imposing duties on designers, manufacturers, importers and suppliers. A chain of responsibility is therefore imposed from the design and manufacture of an article to its installation, use and maintenance. It can be seen, however, that the duties under the Act overlap and this demonstrates the stated aim of the legislation of accident prevention.

The duty owed to employees in that by s 2 of the Act, if the Employer employs five or more persons he should have a general policy on health and safety and bring this policy to the notice of his employees. The policy should identify who is responsible for health and safety and should point out particular health and safety problems and arrangements for dealing with them. The policy should also cover such matters as training and supervision, inspection procedures, safety precautions and consultative arrangements. In addition, it must tell the employee how he can complain about any health and safety risk to which he feels he is being exposed.

While the common law imposes no duty on the employee to look after his own health and safety, failure to do so could mean that any damages could be wiped out by the employer raising the defence of contributory negligence. given that the aim of the statutory duty is not to provide compensation, the Act places a duty on the individual employee to have regard to his own safety and that of those around him. Often, employers will make breach of health and safety regulations a disciplinary offence and in some case it may be fair to dismiss an employee for such a breach. In Rogers v Wicks and Wilson COIT 90/97 willful breach of a no smoking policy imposed for safety reasons was held to be a justifiable reason for dismissal.

Health and Safety Representatives

There is a right under the HSAW for employees to have a safety representative who will in turn report to the employer. Further regulations were introduced and under the Safety Representatives and Safety Committees Regulations 1977, safety representatives should investigate potential hazards and dangerous occurrences at the workplace, investigate complaints from employees relating to health and safety and make representations on these matters to the employer and to the health and safety inspectors. If two safety representatives so request in writing, the employer must establish a safety committee which can keep policy and practice under review. Under the Health and Safety (Consultation with Employees) regulations 1996, employers must consult with employees either directly or else with their elected representatives over the introduction of any measure or new technology which might affect health and safety, appointments under the Management of Health and Safety at Work Regulations 1999 and health and safety information generally. Health and safety representatives are entitled to time off in pursuit of their work.

Health and Safety Regulations and Codes of Practice

The Secretary of State has the power to make regulations, either on the proposal of the Health and Safety Commission or after consultation with it

(HSWA s.15). The most important regulations are the Control of Substances Hazardous to Health Regulations 2002 (COSHH), but other examples include the Health and safety Information for Employees Regulations 1989 and the Noise at Work Regulations 1989.

For an in depth view of current health and safety regulations, which are many and varied, you should go to the Governments Health and Safety website www.hse.gov.uk.

10

The Role of Trade Unions

In the United Kingdom, there is a general freedom to associate, with the exception of the police and the armed forces. The freedom to form and belong to an association, whatever association, is regarded as a fundamental human right. However, as we all know, the history of relations between state and unions, employer and unions has always been fraught with problems.

Most employees (and employers) will be represented by some sort of trade union. Whether or not the trade union is active in the workplace or whether the individual is a member of the relevant trade union is another matter. The 2004 Employment Relations Act is the most recent piece of significant legislation governing relations between employers/employees and Trade Unions.

Definition of a trade union
The statutory definition of a trade union is now found in s1 (a) of the Trade Union and Labour Relations (Consolidation) Act 1992 that provides that a trade union means:

"an organisation (whether temporary or permanent) which consists wholly or mainly of workers of one or more descriptions and whose principle purposes includes the regulations of relations between workers of that description or those descriptions and employers or employers associations."

The definition is wide and concentrates on the purpose of that body. Thus a body which had a subsidiary purpose of regulating relations between workers and employers would not be a trade union.

The Certification Officer

The Certification Officer and Independent Trade Unions

The Certification Officer is the official who maintains a list of trade unions and can issue any union with a certificate of independence. Such a certificate is conclusive evidence that a union is independent. Section 5 of the Trade Union and Labour Relations (Consolidation Act) 1992 states that an independent union is one which is not under the control of an employer or liable to interference from an employer arising out of financial, material or other support. This definition was elaborated in the Court of Appeal and Squib UK Staff Association v Certification officer (1979).

Recognition of Trade Unions

The major purpose of any union is to protect and promote its members interests and the way it will do this is by collective bargaining. Recognised Trade Unions have certain rights. Recognised Trade Unions are entitled to information for collective bargaining purposes. Although there is now no formal way that a union can demand recognition from an employer, recognition procedures having been abolished by the Employment Act 1980, the 1999 Employment Rights Act, coming into force on 6th June 2000, introduced a new right where, if more than 20 people are employed in a company, and a majority of staff are in favour of joining a union, then an employer must recognize that union in the workplace

The Rule Book

The rules of a trade union form the terms of a contract between it and its members. They become part of a contract in the same way that collective agreements become part of the individuals employment contract between the employer and the employee. Apart from contract, other areas of law impact on the union rulebook. Statute has now impacted in a variety of ways. By s 69 of the Trade Union and Labour Relations (Consolidation) Act 1992, for example, there is a rule in union rulebooks allowing a member to terminate his membership on the giving of reasonable notice.

In addition, both the Sex Discrimination Act 1975 and the Race Relations Act 1976 (replaced by the Equality Act 2010) rendered it unlawful to discriminate on the grounds of race or sex, in relation to membership.

The Right to Information

The Employment Protection Act 1975 recognised that to be able to collectively bargain effectively, unions needed certain information from the employer and as such the Act introduced a right to receive certain information. This right has been retained and the provisions are now ss 181-5 of the Trade union and Labour Relations (Consolidation) Act 1992. The employer only has to disclose information in relation to those matters for which the union is recognised for collective bargaining.

ACAS has produced a code of practice (ACAS Code of Practice 2: Disclosure of information to Trade Unions for Collective Bargaining Purposes) which in paragraph 11 lists the type of information it would be good industrial relations practice to disclose. This includes pay and benefits, conditions of service, manpower, performance and financial information. Section 182 of the Act provides restrictions on information that the employer does not have to disclose, such as information in the interests of national security. Section 183 provides a remedy for a trade union where the employer has failed to provide information. The remedy is complaint to the Central Arbitration Committee (CAC). Sections 184-185 further strengthen the complaints procedure.

The Closed Shop

There was no legal control over the closed shop until the Industrial Relations Act 1971. This Act introduced the concept of unfair dismissal. In 1988, the Employment Act 1988 rendered any dismissal for union or non-union membership unfair in any circumstances (now s 152 of the Trade Union and Labour Relations (consolidation) Act 1992.

As such, while post entry closed shops can still exist, no one can be legally compelled to join a union.

The legislation of 1988 however, did nothing to prevent pre-entry closed shops operating, pre entry meaning insistence on membership of a union before being offered employment. The Employment Act 1990 finally destroyed any protection which existed for the pre entry closed shop by rendering it illegal to discriminate on the grounds of membership of a union prior to employment. This is now Ss 137-1243 of the Trade Union and Labour Relations (Consolidation) Act 1992.

Rights of Trade Union members
Enforcement of the Rule Book

While there is a special statutory protection for union members in relation to rules relating to discipline and exclusion and expulsion a member must rely on the common law to enforce any other rule in the rulebook.

Although the rulebook forms the contract of membership between the individual member and union, this will not always provide him with a remedy. Rather, the trade union member is treated in a similar way to a shareholder in a company and as such his remedies against the union are similar to those imposed against incorporated associations.

The simple proposition is that as a union as an entity only exists as a creation of statute, its legal capacity to act comes from its rules and to some extent from statute. As such, if the rules or statute lay down when a union can act then should the union act without fulfilling the requirements it has no capacity to do so and as such its actions are ultra vires.

Exclusion and Expulsion

We have already seen that essentially a trade union cannot legally enforce a closed shop and therefore it may appear that any discussion on exclusion and expulsion may be redundant.

Closed shops still exist, however, in certain industries and whereas the employee may have a remedy against the employer for refusing to employ him because he is not a trade union member, that will not help him if the reason he is not such a member is that the union do not want him or have expelled him.

Discipline of union members

Although expulsion from the union may be imposed as a disciplinary sanction, it is not the only form of sanction imposed by a union on its members. The courts insist however, that the union must comply with the natural rules of justice when exercising sanctions against a member. These are:

1. *Notice.* A person must be given adequate notice of the charge against him and the potential penalty so that he has an opportunity to answer it. In Annamunthodo v Oilfield Workers Union (1961) the plaintiff knew that he was being charged with making allegations against the union presidents and knew he could be fined. He did not know that such conduct was treated as prejudicial to the union and that he could be expelled. It was held that his subsequent expulsion was void.

2. *Opportunity to put his case.* A person must be given the opportunity to put his side of the case and answer any charges against him.

3. *Unbiased hearing.* The hearing should be unbiased.

4. *Representation.* The rules do not specifically state that a person should be allowed legal representation and it appears from Enderby Town Football Club v Football Association (1971) that such representation can

113

be specifically excluded by the rules as long as some kind of representative is allowed.

Action Short of Dismissal

The law affords a certain amount of protection against an employer. The law protects an employee who is dismissed for trade union membership or non-membership or for taking part in trade union activities at the appropriate time. Protection against dismissal is complemented by protection against action short of dismissal for one of the above grounds and is now found in s 146 of the Trade Union and Labour Relations (Consolidation) Act 1992. Should a tribunal find a complaint well founded it can make a declaration to that effect and award compensation to offset any loss caused by the action. In addition, either the complainant or the employer may join the union as a co-respondent if it was union pressure which induced the action and the tribunal can order that some or all of the compensation be paid by the union. Refusal to grant a benefit on these grounds is action short of dismissal for the purposes of protection.

In NCB v Ridgeway (1987) it was held that refusal to give a pay rise negotiated with the UDM to NUM Members was unlawful action short of dismissal. In other words it is sufficient if the employer discriminates against members of a particular union and it is not necessary to show discrimination against union members as a whole.

Industrial Action

The present law on industrial action has had a chequered history. For many years the law was, to a large extent, non-interventionist in this area. The main piece of legislation governing industrial action was the Trade Disputes Act 1906 which created the basic immunities.

Change came with the Conservative Government in the early 70's and the Industrial Relations Act of 1971. The Act introduced a system of registration for trade unions and attacked the closed shop. Since 1979, there have been a number of reforms, ten pieces of legislation in all.

Employment legislation overall is part of broader economic policy, that of the encouragement of market forces. Reduce the power of the unions and you remove the obstacles to competitiveness. The 2004 Employment Relations Act is the latest in a line of legislation designed to regulate activities of trade unions.

Industrial Action and the Contract of Employment

There is no "right to strike" in UK law. Virtually all forms of industrial action will constitute a breach of contract on the part of the employee. There are a number of forms, or types of industrial action. It is important to distinguish between official action and unofficial industrial action. Official action is that which is supported by the trade union and unofficial action is that which the union has not repudiated. For action to be deemed unofficial, it is not sufficient that the union merely does not support it, the union must actively repudiate the action (Express and Star Ltd v NGA (1985)). The main reason for differentiating between unofficial action and official action is that if workers are dismissed for taking part in unofficial action the employment tribunal will have no jurisdiction to hear their complaint of unfair dismissal.

Go Slow

Go-slow is a breach of an implied term to work at a reasonable pace in the absence of justifying circumstances.

Work to rule

The leading case of Secretary of State for Employment v Aslef (1972) decided that such an action could constitute a breach of contract, as the employees were following a rulebook set out by the employer which did not constitute a contract.

Overtime ban

Whether this action constitutes a breach of contract depends on whether the overtime is compulsory or voluntary and involves looking at the terms of the contract itself.

Blacking

This may take a variety of forms. If a reasonable order is given by the employer however, and the employee refuses to undertake the work then this can be seen as breach of contract. Another form of blacking may constitute refusing to work with ones fellow employees.

In Bowes and Partners v Press (1894) miners refused an order to go down in a cage with a non-unionist. It was held that their action was a breach of contract.

Strike without notice

A strike is a situation where an individual withdraws his labor and refuses to work. As such, he is in breach of contract by refusing to work.

Strike with notice

This area is complicated and a number of court cases have tried to determine whether a strike with notice is in fact breach of contract or resignation of the employee.

One leading case is that of Miles v Wakefield Metropolitan District Council (1987) House of Lords where it was held that all industrial action is a repudiatory breach of contract since there is an intention to harm the employers business which goes fundamentally against the duty of loyalty and co-operation which the employee owes to the employer.

If this view is correct and the intention behind the action is one of legality, it would suggest that any strike notice, whether of correct length or not is notice of a breach of contract and it will only be construed as notice to terminate if it is expressed to be so.

Trade Dispute

In terms of legal liabilities, it is of the utmost significance whether an act is done in contemplation or furtherance of a trade dispute' since the statutory immunities discussed below only apply in certain circumstances.

If an act falls outside of a trade dispute, the immunities cease to operate and the full rigour of the law applies.

Section 244 TULCRA defines a trade dispute as '... a dispute between workers and their employer which relates wholly or mainly to one or more of the following, that is to say:

a) terms and conditions of employment, or the physical condition in which any workers are required to work;

b) engagement or non-engagement or termination or suspension or the duties of employment, of one or more workers;

c) allocation of work or the duties of employment as between workers or groups of workers;

d) matters of discipline

e) the membership or non-membership of a trade union on the part of a worker;

f) facilities for officials of a trade union and

g) machinery for negotiation or consultation and other procedures, relating to any of the foregoing matters, including the recognition by employers or employers associations of the right of a trade union to represent workers in any such negotiations or consultation or in the carrying out of such procedures'.

The above definition was introduced in 1982 and the present definition is narrower in two broad respects:

a) it extends only to disputes between workers and their employers. It does not embrace disputes between workers and workers.

117

b) the dispute must relate wholly or mainly to one of the matters mentioned in the 1993 Act.

Industrial action and the economic torts

Inducement of a breach of contract

Since the passage of the Employment Act 1982, trade unions are no longer immune from suit in tort. If a person induces a party to break that contract, the injured party may sue the inducer in tort for inducement of a breach of contract. However, in order to be liable, the defendant must have induced an unlawful act. If the unlawful act is a breach of contract, the contract must exist and be valid in law at the time of inducement. (Long v Smithson) 1918.Knowledge and intention are also necessary requisites for an unlawful act.

Further, the concept of inducement is important here. The word inducement implies pressure being put on an unwilling party, but what amount of inducement does the law require. The key fact seems to be the intention of the person communicating, or the speaker and if that person intends that the contract be broken then there is an inducement even if the speaker is merely communicating a set of facts to the recipient of the information.

Intimidation

The basis of this tort is the use of unlawful threats to induce a party to commit a lawful act, which causes injury, classically, threatening industrial action which causes the employer to lawfully terminate an employees contract. The requirements of the tort are unlawful threats, intention to harm, causation and loss to the plaintiff.

Conspiracy

This tort consists of two forms, the first simple conspiracy to injure and the second to use unlawful means. The existence of a simple conspiracy was recognised in Mogul Steamship v Mcgregor and Co (1892) when the

House of Lords stated that the tort had three elements: a combination of at least two persons; intentionally causing loss; and the predominant purpose is not to further a legitimate interest. In addition, there must be an agreement to injure, not just a co-incidental action.

This is different to criminal conspiracy where the intention to cause loss forms the basis of the offence even if no loss occurs.

Interference with a trade or business by unlawful means

This tort was declared to exist by the Court of Appeal in Hadmor Productions Limited v Hamilton (1981). In Hadmor it was alleged that ACCT officials threatened to persuade their members to refuse to transmit television programmes produced by Hadmor. Thames Television had acquired a licence to transmit the programmes but was under no contractual obligation to do so. Therefore, Hadmor had no contract to breach in this case. It was held, however, that a tort existed. Although the essence of a tort is unlawful means an intention to harm a plaintiff can also be a tort.

Economic duress

All industrial action is intended to put pressure on the employer. In contact law, economic pressure can amount to duress and, if proved, the contract can be avoided and any money paid under it recovered. Normally this argument is not used against unions as they have no contract with the employer. However, in Universe Tankships of Monrovia v International Transport Workers Federation (1983) such a contract did exist. The Federation, as part of its campaign against flags of convenience, insisted that employers pay a sum into the union's welfare fund as the price for lifting the blacking of a ship. As soon as the blacking was lifted the employers sought to recover the money they had paid, arguing the payment had been made under duress and therefore was avoidable. The House of Lords said that if the action had been protected by the immunities, that is, if it was in contemplation or furtherance of a trade dispute, the employer could not circumvent the protection by bringing an action for duress. However, since payment into a welfare fund is not a recognised trade dispute, there was no such protection and the employer's action succeeded.

Statutory Immunities

It can be seen from the above that unions can commit a great number of economic torts when they take industrial action, but we have also seen that in some circumstances there will be statutory immunity from liability for the commission of certain torts. The immunity is now contained in s 219 of the Trade Union and Labour Relations (consolidation) Act 1992, which states: "An act done by a person in contemplation or furtherance of a trade dispute is not actionable in tort on the ground only -

a) that it induces another person to break a contract or interferes or induces another person to interfere with its performance or

b) that it consists in his threatening that a contract (whether one to which he is a party or not) will be broken or its performance interfered with, or that he will induce another person to break a contract or interfere with its performance.

It will be seen therefore that protection is not afforded against the commission of any tort and that such torts as libel and slander, trespass, breach of statutory duty and so on have no immunity.

Trade union liability

The 1906 Trade Disputes Act introduced immunity from tortious liability for trade unions. This blanket immunity was removed by the Employment Act 1982 and now a union has the same immunity as its individual members. There is a statutory limit on the damages that can be awarded against a union, first introduced in 1982 and now contained in s 22 of the 1992 Consolidation Act.

The amount of damages depends on the number of members the trade union has. If there are less than 5,000 the maximum is £10,000. Between

5,000 and 25,000 the maximum is £50,000. Between 25,000 and 50,000 the maximum is £125,000 and over 100,000 the limit is £250,000. Each separate action may result in the maximum being imposed. Therefore, if more than one employer takes action against the union then the limit can be imposed separately for each employer. Furthermore, the limit only applies to damages and not for fines for contempt. Thus in the NGA dispute against the Stockport messenger in 1984 the union was fined £675,000 for contempt.

Loss of trade union immunity
Trade Union Immunity depends on the protected torts being committed and the balloting and notice requirements being complied with. Breach of any of these conditions will render the union liable for any tortious wrongs committed. A ballot is required in respect of any act done by a trade union, that is, in respect of any action authorised or endorsed by the union. Entitlement to vote must be accorded to all members of the union who will be induced to take part in the action and the ballot will be ineffective if this provision is not complied with.

Picketing
Picketing is a method by which a trade union can strengthen a strike. It can prevent workers from entering the workplace and so increase the disruption to the employer. The problem with picketing from a legal point of view is that it involves a consideration of both the civil and criminal law.

The criminal law becomes involved because the fact that picketing involves a group of people standing around can create criminal liability. In addition, pickets will normally interfere with contracts, be committing a trespass and often be committing a private nuisance, so rendering them potentially liable in tort. As such it is necessary to consider all the potential liability and look at the immunity. Criminal liability, for example may be committing the offence of obstructing the highway, obstructing a police officer during the course of his duty or causing a public nuisance generally.

Civil liability might be that of committing a private nuisance, which is unlawful interference with an individual's enjoyment of his land, trespass to the highway or general economic torts such as breach of contract of employment.

Immunity for pickets is contained in s 220 of the 1992 Act. This renders it lawful for a person, in contemplation or furtherance of a trade dispute, to attend at or near his own place of work for the purpose of peacefully obtaining or communicating information, or peacefully persuading a person to work or not to work. In addition, a trade union official may peacefully picket at or near the place of work of a member of the union whom he is accompanying or whom he represents

Unemployed employees are allowed to picket their former place of work if their employment was terminated in connection with the trade dispute or the dismissal gave rise to the trade dispute.

Remedies

Obviously, although the individual member commits the tort, it is more beneficial for an employer to sue the union, hence the removal of blanket union immunity in 1982. The majority of employers, however, do not want damages but rather want to prevent the action from commencing or to stop it as soon as possible. The most common remedy sought is that of injunctive relief. If the union fails to comply with an injunction the two methods of enforcement are committal for contempt and sequestration of the union assets.

The court may imprison for contempt, fine or order security for good behavior.

The 2002 Employment Act-Union Learning Representatives

The 2002 EA, S.43 provides for time off for Union learning representatives. These provisions are similar to time off rights for Health and Safety Representatives. They allow time of for Union appointees, working in the interests of members of trade unions to:

122

- Analyse learning or training needs
- Provide information about or promote learning or training
- Arrange learning or training
- Consult with employers about any of the above

11

Solving Grievances-Tribunals and Arbitration

Before the advent of the industrial tribunal system in 1964, labour law was regarded as an aspect of the law of contract, dealt with by the civil courts. Since 1964, the industrial tribunal system has grown and now encompasses other courts and non-judicial bodies. Industrial tribunals were renamed Employment Tribunals by the Employment Rights (Dispute Resolution) Act 1998. The Employment Tribunals Act 1996 also regulates Employment Tribunals.

The 2002 Employment Act introduced significant proposed changes to the tribunal system along with the Employment Tribunals (Constitution and Rules of procedure) Regulations 2004. In addition, there have been Regulations issued in 2005 and 2008. The President of the Tribunal can also issue new directions from time to time.

Most people with grievances relating to their employment will attempt to resolve these from within, utilising procedures set up by the employer. Usually, policy exists which will encompass most situations, which may arise. However, in some cases, for example, where unfair dismissal is alleged, Employment Tribunals are used.

Employment Tribunals

Employment Tribunals (previously known as Industrial Tribunals) have jurisdiction to hear almost all individual disputes based on statutory employment law claims and, in addition, common law contract claims arising from or outstanding at the termination of employment.

An Employment Tribunal is normally comprised of three members: an ET Judge, being a barrister or solicitor of seven years standing; and two lay members, drawn from either side of industry, one having experience perhaps as a trade union official, the other having had management or trade association experience. Although it is not that common, it is possible for laypersons to outvote the legally qualified chair.

The tribunal system was set up with the aims that it should be quicker, cheaper, more efficient and more accessible than the normal court system. In many ways this has been successful, although delays in processing cases and becoming common, partly due to the increased use of legal representation, particularly by employers, which tends to slow the system down. It is usually recommended, before reaching the stage of going to an Employment Tribunal, that some sort of mediation in the workplace takes place to try to resolve disputes. If this avenue fails then it will usually be necessary to go to an Employment Tribunal. Failure to resolve disputes via mediation, or to attempt the mediation process will not affect rights when going to a Tribunal.

There are a number of advantages and disadvantages to the tribunal system and these include:

a) Informality, lack of ceremony etc. Hearings are normally conducted in a room, which although purpose built, is very similar to any meeting or function room.

b) Representation may be by the party themselves, a lawyer, trade union representative, a friend etc., although it should be noted that most companies tend to be legally represented.

c) Legal aid is not available for first instance tribunal hearings, but may be available for appeal hearings before the Employment Appeals Tribunal (EAT).

d) Costs are rarely awarded, thus there is no financial threat to an applicant bringing a claim.

e) The members of the tribunal are specialist and experienced in employment disputes. Unlike most magistrates or judges, members of an employment tribunal hear only cases within one area of law.

f) Certain rules of evidence, i.e. hearsay, do not apply.

Claims that can be heard by an Employment Tribunal
An Employment Tribunal can only decide cases that relate to specific rights. The range of complaints include:

- Unfair dismissal
- Discrimination on the grounds of disability, race etc.
- Not being allowed to have someone accompany you to a disciplinary or grievance procedure
- Not being consulted in a redundancy situation
- Brach of contract
- Equal pay

There are many others. A full list can be found by contacting ACAS.

The procedure for bringing a complaint before an Employment Tribunal is fairly straightforward. The applicant completes a form and sends it to the tribunal office. A copy of the form is then sent to the employer who has 14 days in which to respond. Both the original form and the employer's response are then copied and sent to the Advisory Conciliation and Arbitration Service (ACAS), who may then attempt to obtain a settlement between parties. If the claim is not settled at this stage, the tribunal will then make a preliminary examination of the case and may hold a pre-hearing review, often consisting of a tribunal judge sitting alone. This is in order to weed out particularly weak cases. Once a case goes to a full tribunal hearing the procedure adopted is similar in many ways to a court hearing, normally being open to the public. It is basically an adversarial procedure, with each party putting its case, witnesses may be called and examined and other evidence produced. However, unlike most other judges in court hearings, the members of the tribunal take a more active role in proceedings, questioning the parties and, if appropriate, leading applicants through the hearing procedure

127

It is now standard practice for the tribunal to give the reasons for its decision in summary form, rather than in extended form, although this does not apply to cases of equal pay or discrimination.

If the applicants claim is successful, the tribunal may award any of three remedies: reinstatement, re-engagement or compensation. The most often awarded remedy is compensation.

How much can the Tribunal award?

(For dismissals and claims post 1 February 2012)

Employment Right	Maximum Award
Unfair Dismissal - Basic Award	£12,900
Unfair Dismissal - Compensatory award*	£72,300
A week's pay	£430 (gross)
Additional award	£11,180-£22,360 (26-52 weeks' pay)
Dismissal for health and safety reasons	No limit
Dismissal for making a protected disclosure (whistle-blowing)	No Limit

Discrimination - Race, sex, disability, sexual orientation, religion or belief and age	No limit
Breach of Contract	£25,000

*N.B. There is no limit on the compensatory award for unfair dismissal where the employee is dismissed unfairly or selected for redundancy for reasons connected with health and safety matters or public interest disclosure

An appeal against a decision of an Employment Tribunal on a point of law only may be made to the EAT. The EAT has a similar standing and many of the same powers as the High Court, and an appeal from the EAT goes to the Court of Appeal, and on occasion from there to the Supreme Court.

The Employment Tribunal is bound by the decisions of the EAT and other superior courts; the EAT, whilst its own previous decisions are only persuasive, is bound by the decisions of the Court of appeal and the Supreme Court.

Further Information

Useful helplines and advice services

TUC Worksmart
Worksmart is the TUC's online information resource providing up to date information and advice on rights at work. This can be accessed via the TUC website wwwtuc.org.uk

http://www.worksmart.org.uk/

TUC Know Your Rights Line
This line will provide you with a range of information.
0870 600 4882

http://www.tuc.org.uk/tuc/rights_main.cfm

ACAS public enquiry points
The Advisory, Conciliation and Arbitration Service (ACAS) is a publicly funded body that promotes good workplace relations: ACAS has a number of advice lines across the country and these can be accessed through directory enquiries.

http://www.acas.org.uk/index.aspx?articleid=1461

The Employment Tribunal Service
0845 795 9775 www.justice.gov.uk

HMRC National Minimum Wage helpline.
0845 6000 678. Further information about the national minimum wage can be obtained from www.hmrc.gov.uk

Low pay unit
General enquiries 020 7721 0450
www.lowpay.gov.uk

Scottish Low pay Unit
0141 221 4491
www.scotlpu.org.uk

Discrimination advice
There are three public agencies that provide advice respectively on sex, race and disability discrimination. They not only provide detailed advice but are prepared to present individual cases. These are:

Commission for Equality and Human Rights
www. equalityhumanrights.com
0845 604 6610

There is also a Lesbian and Gay Employment Rights advice line (LAGER) 020 7704 2205.

The Discrimination Law Association can provide information on discrimination law and promotes access to representation for complainants on 0845 478 6375. www.discriminationlaw.org.uk

Data protection
The Office of the Information Commissioner provides information and advice about the rights of individuals established under the Data Protection Act 1998 and the Freedom of Information Act 2000. tel: 01625 545 745 www.ico.gov.uk

Whistle-blowing
Public Concern at Work can provide advice on 020 7404 6609

http://www.pcaw.co.uk/

Agency Workers
The Department for Business Innovation and Skills regulates employment agencies. Its helpline is 0207 215 0740.

The Recruitment and Employment Confederation (REC) on 020 7009 2100 or at www.rec.uk.com is the trade association for employment agencies. The REC will investigate complaints against those agencies affiliated to it.

Health and safety
The Health and safety Executive information line on 0845 345 0055 can help with all health and safety issues at work.

http://www.hse.gov.uk/

Working time
The Department for Business Innovation and Skills workright number is 0800 917 2368. This helpline will provide information on the working time directive.

The law and advice agencies
The law society is the national body for solicitors. It can give details of local solicitors who can advise on employment matters. 020 7242 1222. www.lawsociety.org.uk

Tax credits and Benefits
You can apply for tax credits online at www.hmrc.gov.uk and this web site also provides extra information about tax credits. There is a special advice line to check your eligibility for tax credits or get a claim pack. There is a helpline for further advice 0845 300 3900 (England, Scotland and Wales) or 0845 607 6078 (Northern Ireland).

Trade Unions

If you want to join or contact a trade union, you can phone the TUC Know Your Rights Line 0870 600 4882 or consult the worksmart website www.worksmart.org.uk

Index

Law

A Straightforward Guide to:

Consumer Rights

Bankruptcy Insolvency and the Law

Employment Law

Private Tenants Rights

Family law

Small Claims in the County Court

Contract law

Intellectual Property and the law

Divorce and the law

Leaseholders Rights

The Process of Conveyancing

Knowing Your Rights and Using the Courts

Producing Your own Will

Housing Rights

The Bailiff the law and You

Probate and The Law

Company law

What to Expect When You Go to Court

Give me Your Money-Guide to Effective Debt Collection

General titles

Letting Property for Profit

Buying, Selling and Renting property

Buying a Home in England and France
Bookkeeping and Accounts for Small Business
Creative Writing
Freelance Writing
Writing Your own Life Story
Writing performance Poetry
Writing Romantic Fiction
Speech Writing
Teaching Your Child to Read and write
Teaching Your Child to Swim
Raising a Child-The Early Years
Creating a Successful Commercial Website
The Straightforward Business Plan
The Straightforward C.V.
Successful Public Speaking
Handling Bereavement
Individual and Personal Finance
Understanding Mental Illness
The Two Minute Message
Guide to Self Defence

Go to:

www.straightforwardco.co.uk